# BUILD YOUR LEADERSHIP MUSCLE

## STRENGTHEN THE LEADER WITHIN



MEETA KANHERE

This is a work of nonfiction. The events and the incidents mentioned in the book are true and real. However, some names and characteristics have been changed, some events have been compressed, and some dialogues have been recreated.



First Edition: January 2026
Printed in India

Printed at: Gapmeta Ventures Pvt.Ltd, Mumbai
Typeset in Adobe Garamond

ISBN: 978-93-6070-683-8

Cover Design: Prajakta Sawant

STORYMIRROR
Stories that reflect you

Publisher: StoryMirror Infotech Pvt. Ltd.
Unit No-F/705, 7th Floor, Kailas Corporate Lounge,
Veer Savarkar Road, Vikhroli Park Site,
Vikhroli West, Mumbai-400079,
Maharashtra, India.

Web: storymirror.com
Facebook: @storymirror
Twitter: @story_mirror
Instagram: @storymirror
Email: marketing@storymirror.com

# DEDICATION

To the leaders who wake up every morning with more questions than answers—yet still choose to show up.

To the ones who carry the weight of teams, deadlines, and decisions, even on days when their own strength feels uncertain.

And to every professional who has ever paused in the middle of a chaotic workday and wondered, *"Is there a better way to lead?"*

This book is born from those questions—and dedicated to you.

# INDEX

# ACKNOWLEDGEMENT

This book carries many stories—some told to me in quiet coaching rooms, some whispered in hurried corridors between meetings, and some shared with vulnerability across conference tables. I owe a deep gratitude to every leader who trusted me with their journeys; your honesty and courage gave this book its heartbeat.

My mentors and fellow practitioners added sparks of wisdom at moments when I needed clarity. My clients offered real situations that shaped the tools and insights in these pages. And my family quietly held the space for me to think, to write, and to return to the keyboard even on days when the words refused to cooperate.

The compilation of this book would not be complete without the dedicated support of Ms. Anuja Chaudhari (who has completed her MBA in Business Analytics in May 2025) from Indsearch, Pune. She not only excels academically but has also received the 'Student of the Year' award for her all-round performance.

My heartfelt gratitude to my mentor, Dr. Jyoti Gogte, who helped me edit this book. As a business mentor, entrepreneur, and author herself, she helped me to develop a reader-friendly approach to the book as well.

To every professional who believes leadership can be learned, practiced, and strengthened—thank you for inspiring this work.

# FOREWORD

**Leadership is often mistaken for visibility, authority, or position.**

In practice, the hardest part of leadership is quieter than that. It shows up in moments of doubt, in conversations people avoid, and in decisions taken without applause.

Over the years, I have seen capable professionals struggle not because they lacked ability, but because no one helped them build the inner strength required to lead others well.

**That is why this book matters.**

I have known **Meeta Kanhere** since her post-graduation days(since 2001) and have observed her grow over the years.

What stands out is the way she has built her craft with care and discipline. She has grown into a **strong facilitator, trainer, and mentor** by paying close attention to **people, behaviour, and learning,** rather than leaning on borrowed language or fashionable models.

*Her credibility comes from staying with the work and learning from it.*

Having worked in leadership and people development for over three decades, I have seen many trainers, coaches, and facilitators at work.

I would place Meeta among the top practitioners I know. What sets her apart is her range. She works comfortably with students who are just beginning to think about leadership, and with CxO-level professionals who carry years of responsibility. That range comes from clarity of thought and genuine respect for the learner, not from titles or authority.

What has stayed consistent through her work is the way she meets people where they are. **She listens carefully, speaks plainly, and takes people seriously.** That quality is felt across her work, and it shapes the way people respond to her.

***Build Your Leadership Muscle*** follows the same approach.

The book does not attempt to impress with complexity, nor does it offer comforting generalities. **Instead, it treats leadership as a skill that must be built deliberately.**

The ideas are practical, the language is accessible, and the intent is clear. It invites readers to stop, think, and take responsibility for how they show up as leaders.

For those stepping into leadership roles, the book helps make sense of the shift from individual contribution to leading others. For experienced managers, it offers something different. It asks questions that nudge them to look again at habits and assumptions that often go unexamined over time.

Leadership today calls for more than execution and expertise. It calls for emotional awareness, steadiness under pressure, and the ability to develop others with intent.

This book stays close to those realities. It does not promise quick results or easy answers. It focuses on what actually makes a difference over time.

**Build Your Leadership Muscle** is best read as a working companion. It is a book to return to at different stages of one's leadership journey. Each time, it offers a chance to strengthen the inner muscle that leadership depends on.

I found this book to be a thoughtful and practical read. More importantly, it reinforces an idea I strongly believe in. Leadership is not about reaching a destination. It is about continuing to grow, make better choices, and increase the impact we have on people and organisations over time.

*Aman Rajabali*

*Leadership Practitioner and Mentor*

*President, National HRD Network, Pune Chapter*

*National Board Member, National HRD Network*

*CEO, Kabir Profile Solutions*

# PREFACE

The idea for this book didn't appear during a perfectly planned moment. It emerged slowly, through countless conversations where leaders said things like:

"People expect me to have it all figured out."

"I know what to do, but I'm not doing it consistently."

"I'm strong in some areas… and surprisingly shaky in others."

Over time, I saw the same truth echoing across industries and hierarchies: **leadership is not a role—it's a rhythm.** Some days it flows effortlessly; other days it stumbles and strains. But just like any muscle, it grows stronger with practice.

*Build Your Leadership Muscle* is a collection of stories, tools, reflections, and small-but-powerful practices. It is not a textbook. It is more like a companion—one that sits beside you during your commute, your coffee break, or your late-night self-reflection and nudges you gently toward a stronger version of yourself.

If leadership feels overwhelming at times, this book is here to remind you: you don't build strength in a day. You build it daily.

# PROLOGUE

Years ago, I sat across from a leader who looked successful in every visible way—sharp, confident, decisive. But that day, he leaned back in his chair and said quietly, "I feel like I've lost my leadership muscle."

That phrase stayed with me. Over the years, I heard it again and again, in different forms:

"I used to be great at empathy."

"I don't know how to influence without authority anymore."

"I've forgotten how to pause."

Every time, the pattern was the same: they hadn't lost the muscle—they had simply stopped training it.

This book begins with that realization. Leadership doesn't vanish; it atrophies. And with intentional practice, it can be rebuilt—stronger, steadier, more authentic.

The pages ahead are filled with the kind of reminders, strategies, and quiet truths that help leaders reconnect with their inner strength, because every leader deserves a comeback—and every comeback begins with one small practice.

# PART 1
# LEADERSHIP AND MANAGEMENT

# INDEX

# SECTION 1: CHAPTERS

# A

# FOUNDATIONS OF LEADERSHIP

## 1. The Essence of Leadership

This is the story of our maid who was planning to visit her village after a gap of almost two and a half years because of the pandemic. She was looking forward to this break and therefore arranged for a replacement. Since she would be on a long break of 3 months, having another maid to do her work was essential. Before she left for her village, she spent an entire week training the new maid in all the housework that she was supposed to do. The maid who would be working as a 'replacement maid' was used to working only on the farm; hence, she had no idea of household chores (like washing, cleaning, sweeping, etc.). But my maid was patient, polite, and effective in the delegation of the work. Besides being specific and clear about the task, she created an encouraging environment. She took feedback from time to time and guided the new maid through this learning journey.

The key message that she was driving through her conversations was 'what to accomplish' rather than just 'what to do.' This established accountability with the new maid. As I had been a silent observer of this journey, I could explicitly see that this was all about her mindset for effective delegation.

**While we can train our leaders to delegate, having the right mindset is the key!**

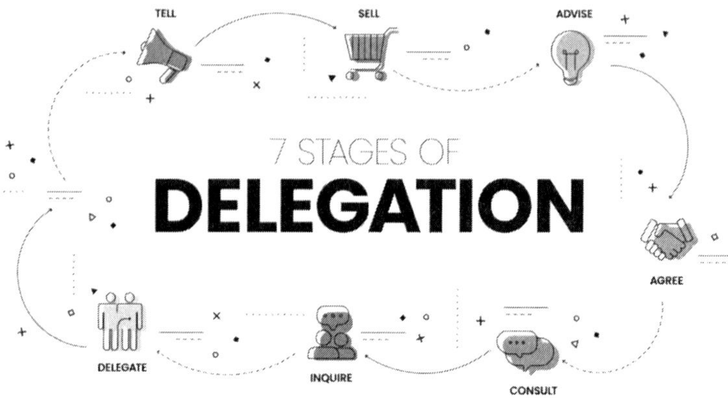


•••

## 2. Chemistry=Mathematics!

One of my earlier bosses was one of the star performers in the company. He said, "Mathematics happens when there is chemistry. The way to achieve those numbers is to create great chemistry with your team members!"

He further added, "Are we ready to understand and connect with our team members? People are always giving us opportunities to tell us something about their lives — are you the manager who can pick up the clues and act on them?"

The leaders can own the entire employee experience by practicing a 10-minute check-in with their team members:

1. How are you doing?
2. How is your team doing?
3. How can I help?

It's very important to connect with your team as 'people' rather than as 'employees' or 'resources'. Along with creating moments of casual conversations, how can one become a better manager?

- Sharing yourself
- Being open to feedback
- Listening to the unsaid

**"Talent will go where it is invited, will perform where it is rewarded, and will stay where it is respected!" Chemistry = Mathematics!**

**DEVELOP TEAM CHEMISTRY!**

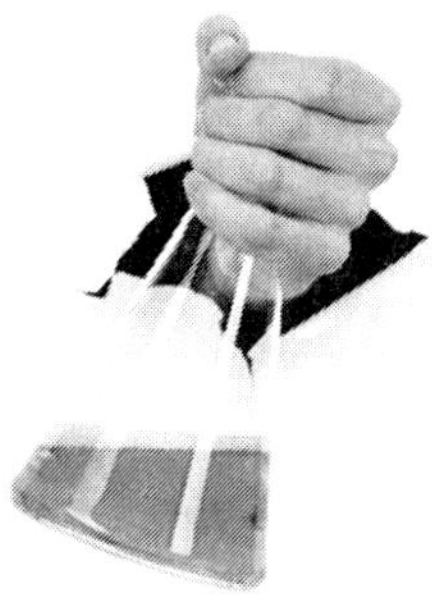

•••

## 3. Identifying and Avoiding Unforced Errors at Work

In tennis, an unforced error is self-induced.

An out-of-court shot or a double fault is regarded as an 'unforced error'.

In a nutshell: a shot that could have been avoided.

At the workplace, the situation is similar. Wrongly informing the successful candidate that they did not make the cut. A stock analyst who inputs a yen amount as a dollar amount by mistake"

In tennis: An unforced error is self-induced. An out-of-the-court shot and a double fault are regarded as 'unforced errors'. In a nutshell: A shot that you could have avoided hitting amiss.

At the workplace, similar is the case. Here are some examples of unforced errors at the workplace:

1. Unjustified assumptions: Making assumptions without sufficient evidence. For example: A firm that assumes a job applicant is a foreign national based on their name alone.

2. Non-compliance: A failure to follow established processes, practices, and procedures. For example: a worker who fails to wear the required safety harness when working at a significant height and ends up falling.

3. Right Thing, Wrong Target: Doing a good job on the wrong thing. For example: Wrongly informing the successful candidate that they did not make the cut

4. Inaccuracy: e.g., A stock analyst who inputs a yen amount as a dollar amount in the valuation model for a Japanese firm.

5. Arriving late at conference calls and meetings.
6. Being unresponsive to email and phone messages.
7. Falling behind on your work, which delays others' progress.

Research shows that even the smartest managers make the worst career errors. Once again, the same is true in tennis. Even the best players in the world make unforced errors in every match. In professional tennis, as in business, the player with the fewest unforced errors usually wins.

**If you want to win and move to the next level, seek a coach!**

•••

B

# CHALLENGES AND GROWTH FOR FIRST-TIME MANAGERS

## 1. Challenges Faced by First-Time Managers

***Most First-Time Managers are in Trouble***

The thrill of a promotion lasts for a little while. But eventually, reality starts to sink in.

Previously, they only had to worry about themselves. Now they live and die by the performance of their team, and that team may consist of people who may not even want to see them succeed.

These managers need help, and they need it fast. Let's look at the cold, hard truth. Brace yourself — this isn't going to be pretty…

***85% of new managers do not get any training prior to becoming a manager. 59% do not feel like they are supported in their new role.***

***63% still do not feel effective after six months on the job.***

***50% still do not feel effective after 12 months on the job.***

Manager training might seem like a no-brainer, but the fact is that companies spend more resources on technical training for managers than they do on training them to lead people. And the results are predictable.

***50% of managers fail during the first year.***

I told you this was going to be scary.

The truth is that half of all first-time managers fail because they are unprepared and untrained. Good intentions aren't enough. They simply aren't ready for the highs and lows that come with managing other adults.

According to research by Gallup, only 1 in every 10 people has what it takes to effectively manage others! Studies and statistics suggest that most first-time managers find themselves lost, underperforming, or even choosing to exit the role in their formative years as a manager.

**If you are a CEO, HR professional, or Head of Department, your first-time managers play a critical role in building a motivated and high-growth team.**

**Investing in their developmental journey is critical.**

•••

## 2. Developing First-Time Managers

In my experience working with several first-time managers who have just risen in the ranks, they need to work in the following areas:

1. **Cultivating a leadership Mindset** - A leadership mindset is a powerful tool for achieving success. It allows leaders to deal with problems and challenges in a way that makes them more likely to succeed. Does the individual have a growth/learning mindset, an accountability mindset, an authentic mindset (self-awareness), and an action-focused (influencing) mindset? The individual should

reflect on all these factors to determine the level of leadership mindset he/she has. Work needs to be done in different degrees for each individual to build a holistic leadership mindset.

2. **Managing Priorities** - The transition from an individual contributor to a first-time manager increases responsibilities on the individual manifold. Managing different priorities: setting goals for team members, delegating, directing and motivating team members, managing performance, building trust and managing conflicts and making decisions could create overwhelming feelings for the individual if he/she is not trained in managing time and priorities well. Along with planning and managing priorities, honing and strengthening each of the above-mentioned skills will also go a long way in helping him/her gain confidence as a first-time manager.
3. **Communicating with Impact** - All the fundamentals of effective communication: expressing with clarity of thought, ensuring understanding of the listener, paraphrasing, giving and receiving feedback, observing and using body language signals to enhance should be sharply focused on. These fundamentals will help in motivating team members, delegating tasks, monitoring performance, managing different stakeholders, influencing and negotiating with them and achieving smoother business outcomes.

**Research shows that organizations investing in training and coaching their first-time managers can experience benefits that have a direct positive impact on business.**

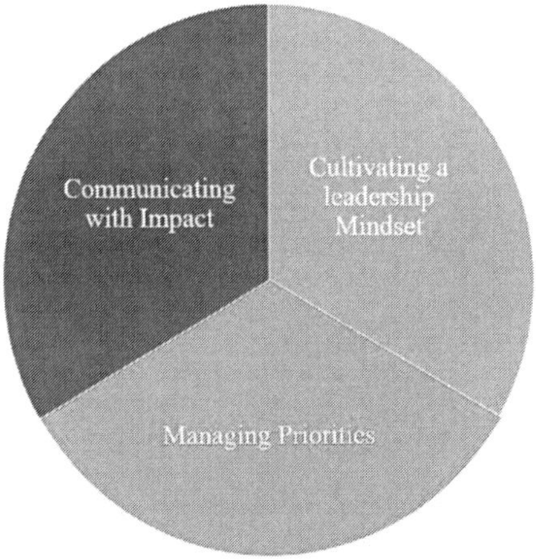


•••

## 3. 90 Day Cheat Sheet for First time managers

***From Individual Contributor to People Leader***

**Core Mindset Shift-** Your role is no longer to do the work yourself, but to enable others to succeed. Measure success by team outcomes, not personal output

| Days 1–30: Listen & Learn | Days 31–60: Align & Enable | Days 61–90: Own & Develop |
|---|---|---|
| **Primary Goal:** Build trust and understand the landscape<br>**What to Focus On**<br>• People before performance<br>• Understanding team dynamics, not changing them<br>• Learning how work really gets done | **Primary Goal:** Create clarity and stability<br>**What to Focus On**<br>• Role clarity<br>• Priorities<br>• Communication rhythms | **Primary Goal:** Step into leadership presence<br>**What to Focus On**<br>• Coaching vs directing<br>• Team capability<br>• Long-term impact |

| **Do This**<br>Meet each team member 1:1<br>**Ask**:<br>• What's working well?<br>• What gets in your way?<br>• How do you prefer to be managed? | **Do This**<br>Set clear expectations<br>• Outcomes > activities<br>• "What does good look like?" | **Do This**<br>Coach for growth<br>**Ask:**<br>• "What's your thinking?" before giving answers<br>• Give regular, specific feedback |
|---|---|---|
| **Observe team dynamics**<br>• Who influences decisions?<br>• Where are bottlenecks?<br>• What's unspoken but obvious? | **Establish team norms**<br>• How do we communicate?<br>• How do we escalate issues?<br>• How do we make decisions? | **Address performance gaps early**<br>• Clear expectations<br>• Clear consequences<br>• No surprises |
| **Clarify expectations with your manager**<br>• Success metrics<br>• Decision authority<br>• Non-negotiables | **Start delegating intentionally**<br>• Delegate outcomes, not tasks<br>• Check understanding, not compliance | **Build your leadership brand**<br>• What will you be known for?<br>• Calm under pressure?<br>• Fairness? Clarity? |
| **Avoid This**<br>• Making quick changes to "prove yourself"<br>• Comparing your style with the previous manager<br>• Over-managing to reduce your own anxiety | **Avoid This**<br>• Doing the work yourself because it's faster<br>• Being the problem-solver for every issue<br>• Avoiding tough conversations | **Avoid This**<br>• Waiting for annual reviews to give feedback<br>• Avoiding conflict to stay "liked"<br>• Micromanaging high performers |

**A Simple Weekly Self-Check**
**Ask yourself:**

- Did I enable or control this week?
- Who did I develop—not just manage?
- What conversation did I avoid?
- What decision could I delegate next time?

**Final Reminder**

Great managers aren't born confident. They become effective by being intentional.

•••

# C

# CAREER DEVELOPMENT AND PERFORMANCE

## 1. Guidance is high, but Development is low

Guidance is high, but Development is low! This was the opinion of a professional about his manager, with whom I was conversing recently. He meant his manager was good at guiding, directing, and supporting him, but when it came to the 'development' aspect, his manager struggled.

Development of a team member can happen in different ways:

1. This can be done by giving timely feedback and helping team members identify current gaps and suggest ways to mitigate them. Feedback is also helpful to reduce gaps between their aspirations and abilities.
2. Creating learning opportunities by deliberately involving the team member in key processes. Learning opportunities can also be created in the following ways:

- Provide training programs employees can take advantage of
- Enable employees to participate in cross-functional projects

- Ask employees to plan company social events
- Have employees lead brainstorming sessions, team meetings, or problem-solving sessions
- Ask employees to mentor new employees
- Task employees with leading process improvement initiatives

3. Nurturing their potential by identifying growth potential and aligning developmental plans accordingly. Start by guiding employees to recognize their strengths and passions, shaping growth opportunities around their areas of expertise. Then, focus on nurturing both their intrinsic qualities—like compassion, collaboration, and confidence—and their external skills, including leadership and professional capabilities. Cultivating strong self-awareness lays the foundation for meaningful growth.

Guiding, supporting, directing are more tactical. However, for developing team members, one needs to cultivate a growth mindset.

•••

## 2. Go beyond perception for conducting meaningful career development conversations

**Perception is reality. If you are perceived to be something, you might as well be it because that's the truth in people's minds ~ Steve Young**

I will use the 360-Degree Feedback Report as a 'Bible' when I am conducting the performance appraisal of my team member. After all, more than 6 stakeholders have spent their time on several questions giving feedback to this team member. Also, isn't this report most important when we have spent so much time and energy to seek perceptions of different stakeholders, and then we don't use it during appraisal?

These were the thoughts of a participant when I was recently conducting a Train-the-trainer (TTT) program on how to do a 360-degree report debrief and conduct career development conversations with their team members. He was so absorbed in the thought that if many people are perceiving something about person 'X', it must be considered as the only piece of evidence for understanding his performance and his developmental journey thereafter.

To understand someone's performance, there are many more factors behind his/her performance (Internal factors such as his/her ability and personal traits, knowledge and skill, willingness to learn; and external factors such as setting clear goals and expectations, giving the right kind of motivation and incentives, tools and resources, and organizational culture). The culmination of both these factors results in someone's performance. So, while conducting a career development conversation, one must take into consideration the internal as well as external factors.

A 360-degree feedback report is a 'perception report', which can be an additional data point to understand if there are any perception gaps in the self vs. others' ratings. The competencies which have come out as 'blind spots' or 'hidden strengths' should be taken into consideration while conducting a career development conversation.

To summarize, perception cannot be the only factor to determine someone's performance and career development path. It can be one data point along with several other important factors as shared above that also need to be considered to curate a meaningful career development conversation.

•••

## 3. Are you creating a safe space for your underperformers?

After attending the 'sangeet' at a wedding recently, I was speaking to the group of girls who gave an awesome dance performance. Clearly there were some amazing dancers, a few mediocre, and the remaining were struggling even with their basic steps. Some of them were lacking in confidence, some lacking in skills. I happened to chat with their leader, and was conversing with her about how she choreographed the whole piece when there was such a big mix of performers. She shared her thought with me, saying that everyone should get an opportunity to come to the center of the stage at least once, so that they get an opportunity to be seen by everyone in the audience. Otherwise, how would they ever overcome the fear they have, and develop the much-required confidence! She further said that it was okay to make a mistake or two, but giving them the opportunity was important. She always had the choice to keep the poor dancers behind the best dancers, but she chose not to.

Learning can be found in every corner of our lives. Likewise, as leaders, when was the last time you-

- gave an opportunity to someone in your team who was struggling with a set of certain skills
- allowed someone to make a mistake
- encouraged someone to try out something new
- held hands patiently so that they overcame their fear to learn something new

**These actions can be the real 'game-changers' when leaders practice them with the best intent.**

•••

# D

# BUILDING TEAM CULTURE

## 1. Empowering Teams Through Trust and Accountability

**Vulnerability is about sharing our experiences and feelings with people who have earned the right to hear them. ~ Brené Brown**

Andy Crouch, an American author and speaker, has presented a 2x2 matrix that he calls the Authority and Vulnerability Paradox in his book Strong and Weak. The vertical axis represents authority or "the capacity for meaningful action". What most people normally think of when they refer to power is the ability to influence events and control circumstances or possess the knowledge or position to do so. However, flourishing only happens when authority is combined with what is sometimes thought to be weakness—vulnerability, defined as "exposure to meaningful risk". This kind of vulnerability is not simply emotional transparency. Crouch summarizes: "True vulnerability involves risking something of real and even irreplaceable value".

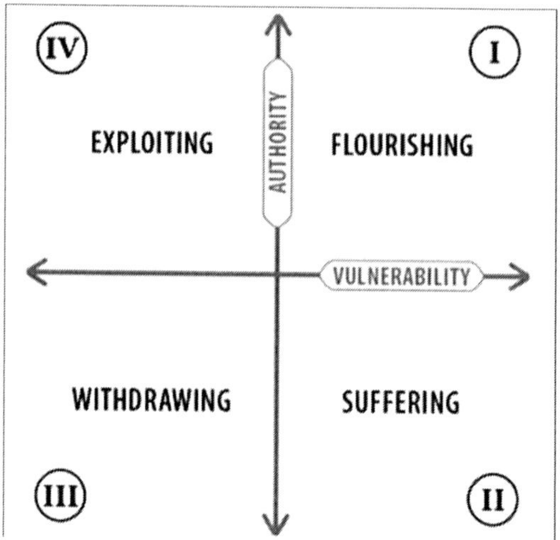


The matrix created by the axes of authority and vulnerability results in four separate quadrants (clockwise from high noon): Flourishing, Suffering, Withdrawing, and Exploiting. The bottom right represents low authority with high vulnerability. This is suffering—experiencing pain without the capacity to change the circumstances. The bottom left is low authority with low vulnerability. This is withdrawing—escaping choices in fear of their consequences. The top left, summarized as exploiting, is the realm of dictators and tyrants—high authority with low vulnerability. Most people are tempted toward this corner when they use authority to reduce vulnerability.

However, flourishing occupies the top right—high authority combined with high vulnerability. When people live in this quadrant, they and their community benefit. Risks are embraced. Leaders develop humility. Control is released. Confrontation results in transformation. Flourishing in a relational sense is the condition that is sometimes referred to as love.

"This is what love longs to be: capable of meaningful action in the life of the beloved, so committed to the beloved that everything meaningful is at risk. If we want flourishing, this is what we will have to learn".

The matrix is a tool to help people understand the relationship between authority and vulnerability in their lives. Crouch argues that authority and vulnerability are not mutually exclusive, but rather go together at the moments of greatest flourishing in our lives. He suggests that we should neither withdraw into safety nor grasp for power but instead embrace both authority and vulnerability to achieve true flourishing.

**As a leader, where do you see yourself in the chart?**

**What is helping and hindering you as a leader from an authority and vulnerability perspective?**

## 2. Motivating Teams through Leadership

As a leader, are you aware of the three powerful ways to stimulate intrinsic motivation in your team members?

1. **Autonomy:** A person can only be intrinsically motivated when he or she feels that he or she has the autonomy to choose. The decision to engage has to be a "free choice" with no strings attached.

   To help you increase autonomy in your team, how often do you allow team members to decide how to achieve goals? You may be providing resources, tools, and training, but do you let team members choose what they need and how to use them?

2. **Sense of Competence:** One of the biggest intrinsic motivators is a sense of competence. When a person completes a difficult task or masters a new skill, he or she feels accomplished and is more likely to do it again. As a leader, how are you supporting them in this journey?

3. **Relatedness:** Another factor that can impact intrinsic motivation is relatedness, which refers to how well one

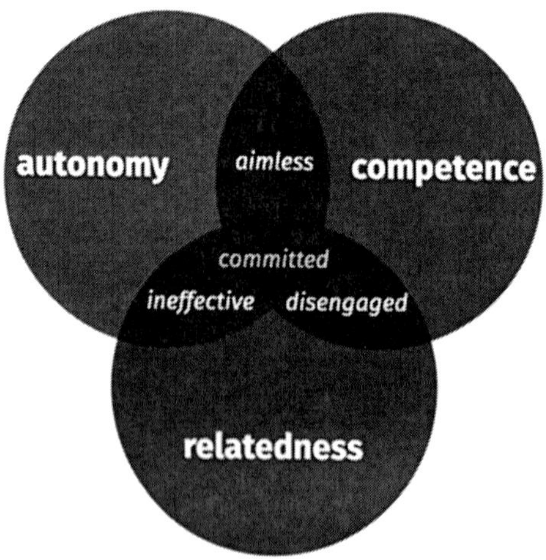

feels connected, secure, respected, and cared for. A leader can create a sense of relatedness through the way he communicates and connects with team members.

Motivating team members is an art.

**"Leaders should spend time with each team member to apply different strokes for different folks."**

•••

## 3. Demonstrating care is essential!

Care demonstrated in times of crisis is often shown by most people, as it may be the need of the hour. However, care as an innate quality, irrespective of the situation, whether in ordinary or crisis, is a rare quality. As a leader, the way one demonstrates care can be a game changer not only in building trust with people but also in influencing their outcomes.

So how can you show you care? Here are three ways:

1. **Get personal:** Show interest in people's lives. Ask questions and really listen. Remember important information such as birthdays, anniversaries, the names of family members, important events in the lives of your team. Write them down, if that helps. But above all, make a personal connection with every member of your team. Stretch yourself to learn something new about someone every day. Meet new team members as they come on board. And if this puts you outside your comfort zone, that's okay. Stretch yourself and make a point of doing it anyway. The end result will be a more engaged team.
2. **Connect the dots:** Ask your employees what they believe their impact is on the organization. Share with them the impact you know they make. We all want to know that

what we do matters, that our time, energy, and creativity add up to something important. Help each person who works for you see the difference they make. They'll be more invested in the work and achieving the big goals.

3. **Measure what matters:** Most things that are being measured at work are meaningless for individual team members. The bottom line is helpful for senior leaders and investors, but not so much for a front-line supervisor. Help your employees measure what matters to them. How can they know at the end of a day that they were successful? What can they measure? For example, if you are in the customer service business, you might measure the number of customers touched in any given day and the number of smiles, good interactions, and outcomes that happened. Coming up with the metrics that matter will take some time with each one of your employees, but it will be worth it.

**Showing your team you care doesn't have to add a bunch to your plate. But it does have to be a priority in your days. Start small and learn as you go.**

**It will make all the difference.**

•••

# E

# HANDLING DIVERSE MINDSETS

## 1. As a leader, how do you tackle and respond to team members with different mindsets?

**Get to know each person on your team. The more you understand each person you have on staff, the more efficient your team is. Take time to interact with each employee to build high-quality relationships.**

1. **Understand each role in your company.** Part of knowing how to manage a team with different personalities is knowing what strengths each role requires. If a team member's role is client-facing, that person will need to have extroverted personality traits. If a role is heavily technical, that person will need to be a natural problem solver. When you understand what is asked of each role, you can hire strategically, incorporate complementary personalities into a team and reduce friction when working with different personalities.

2. **Model empathetic communication.** Great leaders lead by example, especially when they're mastering how to manage a team with different personalities. Demonstrate effective teamwork by tailoring your own communication to the person you're interacting with. If you know they tend to be soft-spoken, be extra sensitive when conversing with them. If they tend to be very direct, approach the conversation with equal directness.
3. **Adopt the situational leadership style** (telling, selling, participating or delegating) in which a leader adapts his or her style of leading to suit the needs of each team member. This style of leadership is not dependent on the skills of a leader; rather, it is based on a leader's ability to adjust to the requirements of a team or organization in order to be a better and more effective leader.

**What more would you add to this list?**

•••

## 2. Leading with Gen Z, and preparing Gen Z to lead

**Every generation changes the workplace. Gen Z is doing it faster—and forcing leadership to evolve.**

The real question isn't *"How do we manage Gen Z?"*

It's **how do leaders adapt—and how does Gen Z prepare—to lead together?**

### What Leaders Must Rethink

Gen Z doesn't follow titles. They follow **authenticity**.

They expect:

- Clear why, not just clear tasks
- Frequent feedback, not annual reviews
- Purpose that's lived, not laminated on walls

The leaders who succeed with Gen Z:

- Coach more than they command
- Set clear boundaries while offering flexibility

*Authority today is earned, not assumed.*

**What Gen Z Must Learn as They Step into Leadership**

Leadership is not just voice—it's responsibility.

As Gen Z professionals grow into leadership roles, the shift is critical:

- Build trust before challenging systems
- Learn to have uncomfortable conversations
- Balance confidence with competence
- Manage up, not just down

*Leadership is influence with accountability.*

**The Leadership Shift That Truly Matters**

The future of leadership is **intergenerational**.

- Senior leaders must move from control to connection
- Gen Z leaders must move from expression to execution

When curiosity replaces judgment, leadership becomes a shared capability—not a generational conflict.

**For Leaders:**

What belief about "how leadership should look" might you need to unlearn to truly engage Gen Z?

**For Gen Z Professionals:**

Are you building leadership *credibility*—or only visibility?

Leadership isn't about age.

It's about awareness, adaptability, and accountability.

•••

# SECTION 2: CASE STUDIES

# A

# TRANSITIONING INTO LEADERSHIP

## 1. Case Study: Challenges of a First-Time Manager

Sheela was promoted to a software development manager position. She had demonstrated strong ideas and performance as a project leader, and Priya, her boss, expected her to excel when she had her own people reporting to her. But Priya didn't recognize a problem Sheela had with self-confidence and prioritization.

As a project leader, she had made effective decisions, and she seemed to cope well with the decision-making process. But apparently her confidence in her project leader's decisions was bolstered by the fact that her manager had the final word on those decisions. Once she moved into the managerial role, she began to second-guess herself. She couldn't adequately prioritize her time between the important decisions and the trivial ones, and she lost her self-confidence.

She got to the point where she would decide something, tell her employees, then change her mind after talking to someone else. Many of those decisions were trivial enough that they didn't significantly affect project success, but it was unproductive to keep changing her mind, and it began to cause a lot of rework.

Priya talked to Sheela numerous times about the problem, but she was unable to regain the focus she had as a project leader. Eventually her stress level got too high, and we decided to ask her to step down from the position.

Situations like the one shared above can become very sensitive and tricky to handle. Rather than having conversations after the problems start to surface, it's best way to take proactive steps by training your first-time managers and making them aware of the changes in responsibilities, values and skill sets required for the role.

**Lessons Learned:**

________________________________________

________________________________________

________________________________________

________________________________________

________________________________________

•••

## 2. Case Study: An over-confident Manager!

Krishna had been very successful in leading infrastructure projects with well-defined objectives. The organization needed a services manager to oversee the infrastructure for a large department, and Krishna was promoted to the position because he was respected by his peers and customers and had good communication skills.

He had the technical background to understand the area he was responsible for, and he worked well with the employees who reported to him. He initially did well in the position, taking care of infrastructure needs and prioritizing work based on the needs of the business.

Over a period of several months, however, he began to get overconfident. The customers for his services began to complain that he wouldn't listen to them, and when his boss had complaints about him, he took the position that he understood their needs better than they did. His boss tried various approaches to improve his customer relationships. His boss also tried working with him on defining customer expectations and on better communication.

Ultimately, however, he couldn't get Krishna to understand that he needed to redefine success to include customer perception. Krishna was removed from the position and transferred to another area that was more project-focused.

The biggest unknown about promoting someone into a first-time manager position is how it will affect the new manager's self-perception. Like Krishna, some let the new implied status and power go to their heads, become overconfident, and don't pay enough attention to the views of their customers and employees. Both reactions can be temporary and can be corrected with time. But different situations demand different levels of tolerance. Sometimes the person has to be taken out of the position if it doesn't appear that the situation can be corrected in the time available.

**Lessons Learned:**

______________________________________________

______________________________________________

______________________________________________

______________________________________________

______________________________________________

•••

## 3. Case Study: Transitioning to a First-Time Manager

Saurabh was a sales executive who was promoted to the post of Sales Manager, as he had been achieving his targets consistently for the last 4 years. The management felt that he was capable and now ready to lead a team of sales executives. This transition from being an individual contributor to a manager calls for changes in one's mindset right from one's mindset to the way one gets things done through others.

Saurabh struggled in this transition, so he continued doing his old role—that of meeting new customers and getting into action. He felt that when one sees him in action, everyone will think that he is working and is busy. (In reality, he was hiding from his new role—and staying within his comfort zone) Of course, this could not sustain for long—and when he was asked for results, he was stuck.

In real life, we find many organizations where individual contributors are promoted to lead a team; however, very few organizations proactively help them to prepare for the new roles and responsibilities they are expected to handle. Handholding, training and coaching first-time managers not only help them gain confidence but also builds their competence to get results through others.

**Lessons Learned:**

________________________________________

________________________________________

________________________________________

________________________________________

________________________________________

•••

# B

# LEADERSHIP APPROACHES AND STYLES

## 1. Case Study: Exploring Different Leadership Styles - What is the impact of my leadership style on my team?

This is a story of a logistics company for whom I was delivering leadership training a few months back. Now, this company wanted to be the market leader and was very aggressive in the way it conducted business. This story is an experience shared by Prasad who was an employee of this organization.

During the training, we were discussing the different leadership styles and their impact on team members. Prasad approached me during the break and shared his experience of working with his boss who had an 'avuncular' approach to working with his team. Because of this approach, he was very nurturing, helpful and kind towards team members; however, he was not at all comfortable when it came to giving feedback or having performance conversations with them. Prasad did not feel engaged on the job, because he felt his growth was somewhat curbed, as he did not receive feedback about his development areas or opportunities for performance enhancement. He also knew that his manager would be retiring in a few months and when a new manager comes in, he will expect Prasad to know things and his worry was that his current boss was not helping him to grow, develop, and give feedback. Hence, he wanted to look out for new opportunities right away.

As a leader, your leadership style has tremendous impact (both positive and negative) on the team. When leaders create a great employee experience, it has a transformative effect on the organization. Your self-awareness not only helps you in your leadership journey but also enhances the team's engagement and productivity.

**Lessons Learned:**

________________________________________

________________________________________

________________________________________

________________________________________

________________________________________

●●●

## 2. Case Study: Can the #weakness of an individual in one context be a #strength in another?

Well, the answer is yes, it can be, if the organization knows how to leverage this and has the right opportunity to do so.

Here's a story of a professional, Rohan, who used to lead a team of managers and his style of managing was rather autocratic. He used to follow up with each and every team member for the minutest of tasks. Over a period of time, the team members were frustrated with his leadership style and escalated the matter to the top leadership. The top team understood the challenge and decided to take an important step which would not only benefit Rohan, but also his team members and the organization. They rotated him to another department, Supply Chain Department, where his primary role was to get in touch with vendors to get things done on time. For Rohan, following up and getting things done was second nature. He readily agreed to move to this role. From a manager's role, he was moved to an individual contributor role. Although Rohan had to step down to an individual contributor role, the organization explained to him that his quality can be leveraged better in this role than the earlier one. The Supply Chain benefited tremendously because of this move, since there was no capable person until then to do that job. The earlier team got a new leader who was more mature in his leadership style while dealing with them. And overall, the organization also benefited because of this change.

While #job rotation was a 'possible solution' in the scenario shared above, can you think of or share any other context where an individual's weakness has been utilized as his/her strength?

**Lessons Learned:**

_______________________________________________

_______________________________________________

_______________________________________________

_______________________________________________

_______________________________________________

•••

# C

# LEADERSHIP GAPS AND PITFALLS

## 3. Case Study: The Pitfalls of Absentee Leadership

Paresh has been leading a team of sales executives for over four years now. In the last few years, although he holds the title of manager, he has been psychologically, emotionally, or even physically absent from his responsibilities. He may be present in the office, but he has been conspicuously absent from meetings, discussions, and decision-making processes. He may hold a title that signifies authority, but he fails to exercise this authority in ways that provide direction, feedback, and support to his subordinates. This absence is not merely a disregard of duty; it is a form of leadership failure that can have far-reaching consequences.

Much like a silent predator, this form of leadership (or lack thereof) can go undetected for extended periods, gradually eroding team cohesion, employee morale, and productivity. Absentee leadership refers to leaders who, despite their physical presence, remain emotionally and psychologically disengaged from their roles and responsibilities. Unlike more overtly harmful leadership styles, such as autocratic or micromanaging styles, absentee leadership does not cause immediate, noticeable damage. Instead, it quietly stifles growth, innovation, and motivation, leading to long-term detrimental effects.

Organizations must roll out initiatives consistently to identify absentee leaders and take the right corrective actions.

**Lessons Learned:**

________________________________________

________________________________________

________________________________________

________________________________________

________________________________________

•••

## 4. Case Study: Navigating Senior Stakeholders

The requirements were gathered over a two-week time period at the start of the project. The project is near completion – the portal has been developed by the IT/Application Development group. It has been tested and will be rolled out early next week. Sarah was approached by a member of the senior leadership team who suggested that it would be of value to add one more component so that employees can also manage a few other features.

Sarah has had such an experience with this senior leadership team stakeholder in the past. Specifically, he has asked for additional scope for projects at the last minute and has been insistent about getting his requirements included, regardless of the cost. In nearly every situation, the project has not been successful, and Sarah has had to answer for the fact that the project was not successful.

- How could Sarah manage this stakeholder?
- How should Sarah avoid this situation in the future?

**Please write your response:**

______________________________________________

______________________________________________

______________________________________________

______________________________________________

______________________________________________

•••

# D

# PERSONAL FACTORS INFLUENCING LEADERSHIP

## 1. Case Study: Is there a connection between childhood experiences and behaviour at the workplace?

I have been a student of Psychology and Organizational Behaviour for more than 18 years. And in most of my interactions with people across sectors I can closely see the connection between their psychological make-up and behaviour at the workplace.

Here are two such cases about Sakshi and Chris. (names changed)

Sakshi had grown up in a 'not-so-happy' family. She had seen many quarrels between her parents and eventually she saw them separating in her early teenage years. She had also seen her father play the 'victim card' in their quarrels and how he blamed her mother for all that had happened. As years went by, Sakshi grew up, completed her education and joined the workforce. Sakshi was a high performer at the workplace and quickly rose in the ranks because of her technical skills. In recent times, when I was interacting with Sakshi's leader, he shared with me about her family and career journey so far and how the past has impacted her personality. Today when Sakshi is as a leader, she unknowingly plays the 'victim card' and puts the blame on her team members in different contexts. When her leader pointed this out to her, she was in denial and it was difficult for her to accept. But when her team members also gave her this feedback, she was stumped. Although she did not quickly accept this in front of them, she at least started thinking about it.

In the second case, Chris was the youngest of four siblings in the family. One of his siblings was mentally challenged and his father had passed away early in life. He felt it was his duty to help his mother in the household, by supporting her in any way he could, after his father passed away. He took up odd jobs as he completed his schooling and graduation. When he entered the workforce after that, he rose in the ranks because of both his technical and people skills. He was a keen learner and at the same time could wear a coaching hat for his peers. In recent times, when his leader shared his early life experiences with me, I was stunned. When I interacted with Chris during the leadership development journey, one could not overlook his enthusiasm, optimism in embracing new things and his ability to go beyond his job description.

Two starkly opposite experiences, but the impact it left on both Sakshi and Chris was entirely different. Our personality is shaped by both nature and nurture. However, the way the individual molds and navigates it in later life is based on self-awareness and how they use it for their growth.

**Lessons Learned:**

________________________________________

________________________________________

________________________________________

________________________________________

•••

# E

# COMMUNICATION AND CONFLICT

## 2. Managing Difficult Conversations

Rajeev, who was the team leader of almost 40 team members, wanted to build up his second-in-line. For this, he had picked Ravi, who had been a consistent high performer in the team and had a great attitude towards work while working with the team. Rajeev had groomed him over a period of time and Ravi was ready to take over the new role as the time for organizational restructuring was approaching. However, fate had some other plans for Ravi when suddenly he went into a coma and had to be hospitalized for a long time. After about 3 months or so, he was returning to normalcy. However, the recovery did not bring back 100% of his memory, and he could not perform up to his full potential.

Now Rajeev was completely disheartened because he had put all his time and energy into grooming Ravi and fate was showing a totally different picture of him. The top management asked Rajeev to have a tough conversation with Ravi, asking him to leave the organization because the role demanded much more from him and there was no other suitable role in the organization to which he could be transferred. With a heavy heart, Rajeev navigated these conversations sensitively and it took almost three to four conversations for Ravi to understand the hard reality.

Today, when I was talking to Rajeev, he spoke about still being in touch with Ravi, who is working in another organization. This has been a journey of sorts for both, and the best part was that the transition happened without leaving a bad taste.

How do you deal with a team member who is going through tough times?

**Please write your response:**

# SECTION 3: ACTIVITY

# LEADERSHIP & MANAGEMENT

**Objective:**

Enhance a manager's leadership and decision-making skills by reflecting on daily challenges and evaluating the manager's responses.

Instructions:

**1. Keep a Leadership Journal:**

For one week, the manager records key decisions he or she makes each day

| Particulars | Monday | Tuesday | Wednesday | Thursday | Friday |
|---|---|---|---|---|---|
| 1. What was the situation? | | | | | |
| 2. What decision was made? | | | | | |
| 3. What factors influenced the choice? | | | | | |
| 4. What was the outcome? | | | | | |
| 5. What could have been done differently? | | | | | |

**Self-Assessment:**

- At the end of the week, review journal entries.
- Identify patterns in decision-making, strengths, and areas for improvement.

Reflection Questions:

A. Did I delegate effectively?

B. How did I communicate my expectations?

C. How did my team respond to my leadership?

D. Were there any unforced errors I could have avoided?

E. What will I change next week?

- "Write about a time you handled a team member with a different mindset."
- "What leadership habit are you actively trying to improve?"
- Take a 30-day challenge to reflect on your progress.

Why This Activity?

- Encourages self-awareness and continuous improvement.
- It helps managers track their growth and identify patterns in leadership style.

•••

# PART 2
# PERSONAL DEVELOPMENT AND SELF-AWARENESS

# INDEX

## Part 2: Personal Development and Self-Awareness

# SECTION 1: CHAPTERS

# A

# THE LEADERSHIP LENS

## 1. Leaders' Challenges

In my recent interactions with several leaders, some of the challenges that they experience are:

Lack of self-awareness in understanding their own strengths and developmental areas. How one leverages strengths or manages developmental areas is a gap that I saw in many leaders. This also manifests as overconfidence or underconfidence in their demeanor. When overconfidence was demonstrated, team members perceived it as aggressive behavior and when underconfidence was demonstrated, team members perceived it as submissive behavior.

While most leaders may be aware of the big picture, many tend to struggle to know the ground realities. Many of them speak about inadequate time at hand to know the finer details of the market situation or spend time with different stakeholders or make time for one-on-ones with team members. Many leaders also talk about a lack of skills to connect with their team members. Reasons could be varied and unique to each one of them; however, the consequences would be multifold.

Managing Generation Z: There is an inability to understand their hunger, ways of working, or approach. Most of the leaders struggle to know the best ways to motivate the young folks to give their best. At times, they may also struggle to help them understand the connection between their goals and the organizational goals.

**As a leader, are you facing any of these challenges?**

•••

## 2. Have You Reflected on How Leaders Impact You?

They impact us at many levels - conscious, subconscious, and emotional levels as well. Once we are aware of this aspect, we may be able to navigate our journey in an impactful way. Last weekend, I did a reflective exercise and actually wrote down the qualities of the leaders I have worked with in the past. They have played a valuable role in shaping my professional journey. Here are some qualities that I wrote down as I reflected. (Not in chronological order)

**Leader 1:**

Good Qualities: humility, patience, ever-smiling, building credibility through competence

Bad qualities: not aggressive in approach, content with the work he or the company could attract, very soft in his approach with team members

**Leader 2:**

Good Qualities: attention to detail, perfectionist, timeliness, readiness to learn, subject matter expert, thoroughly professional, ability to look at all perspectives in difficult situations, ability to attract work because of subject matter expertise.

Bad qualities: micromanagement, complete taskmaster, overly critical; could dampen others' confidence at times!

**Leader 3:**

Good Qualities: strategic thinker, a rounded professional experience (corporate and academic), knowledge beyond his core subject, a voracious reader, and encouraging others to be open to learning.

Bad qualities: Using people strategies which created favoritism and inner groups, and at times impacting people dynamics.

**Leader 4:**

Good Qualities: Good administrator, following laid down systems well, and at the same time building in pathways to navigate different projects

Bad qualities: low on confidence

**Leader 5:**

Good Qualities: Highly competent in his subject matter, ability to use data, technology, an awesome problem-solving approach. Despite having a technical background, he was good at behavioral sciences too. Ability to write emails on 'difficult topics' was a great differentiator in his communication. Willingness to learn new skills and upgrade himself. Persistent in getting things done.

Bad qualities: Inability to handle anger tactfully. Extremely shrewd professional, which could come in the way of relationships with different stakeholders.

Looking back, I think I was able to categorize their good and bad qualities more clearly than when I was working with them. There are some leaders who have left a profound impact on my professional journey in terms of thought, approach to working and getting results. What not to do, especially in difficult situations has been tough, yet a great lesson as well!

•••

## 3. Are You Aware of Your Bias?

I was stumped! An eye-opening scene! How a coaching conversation can become a 'breaking your bias' moment!

A virtual BEI (behavioral event interview) was scheduled last month with one of my clients. I was going to meet a Senior Director of an organization and interview him for a set of competencies and evaluate his readiness for promotion. Despite being aware of the "breaking your bias," my mind started creating a visual of this person whose details I had received (name, years of work experience, designation etc.) My internal talk was: Meeta, please keep the details aside and focus on the conversation without getting biased. This person was from a different caste and there lay my bias, which was almost painting the entire picture of the conversation darkly.

Right from the moment the conversation started, my attention was drawn to his 'down to earth' approach of rising in his career, starting from scratch and building teams across organizations he had worked for to date, the kind of connection he was able to establish with different stakeholders was impactful and wouldn't go unnoticed. These and many other experiences that he shared, were constantly a reminder for me to look at the whole person and listen with unbiased thoughts. He busted my bias through his demeanor and communication style. The authenticity with which he shared his experiences was commendable. At the end of the conversation, I was happy to have learned a lot from him in the most 'unassuming' way.

•••

# 4. Is It OK to Be Vulnerable as a Leader?

Why vulnerability is the first thing you look for in other people, but the last thing you want to reveal in yourself.

**Let's try to address some myths about being vulnerable.**

**Myth #1: Being Vulnerable Means Being Weak**

While vulnerability does stem from situations that make you feel afraid, it's important to understand that vulnerability isn't fear. Rather, it's recognizing your feelings of fear and knowing that something out of your control may happen and being brave enough to push on anyway. Walking into, rather than avoiding, tough situations or the potential for failure is not weak; it takes an immense amount of courage.

**Myth #2: I Don't Need Anyone**

Asking for help, sharing ideas, and connecting with others can be frightening because you can't control how your need for help or your ideas are perceived, or you may be rejected. You can avoid this vulnerability only if you never connect with or depend on anyone, but of course, this isn't a plausible choice in an innovative work culture where collaboration is crucial. Humans are social by nature—we depend on the ability to communicate, work together, and depend on one another in order to thrive. Fearing, and subsequently refusing, this collaborative part of our nature can cause innovative cultures to collapse.

**Myth #3: Vulnerability in Leadership Means expressing Everything**

Practicing vulnerability as a leader does not mean expressing all your emotions and personal details. Instead, brave leaders practice vulnerability by acknowledging the uncertainty or risk of a situation, talking openly about the emotions tied to it, and creating a space where your team members feel safe discussing it. This might look like:

***"Our organization is undergoing a lot of changes. It's normal to be anxious during this time—I'm right there with you. What questions or concerns do you have? How can I support you through this?"***

Asking for input from your team members, thereby building a safe space for discussion, is crucial to encouraging vulnerability among your team. Without fear of backlash, they're more likely to ask questions, propose new ideas, or admit mistakes. Be sure that your team members fully understand what the objective of this space is. Having safe spaces does not mean they won't face any pressure or problems. The creation of a safe space for discussion does not mean that when pressure or problems come up, the tough conversations surrounding them will necessarily happen face-to-face and honestly. There won't be gossip at the water cooler or leaked information among colleagues.

**As a leader, how could you encourage appropriate vulnerability in your teams?**

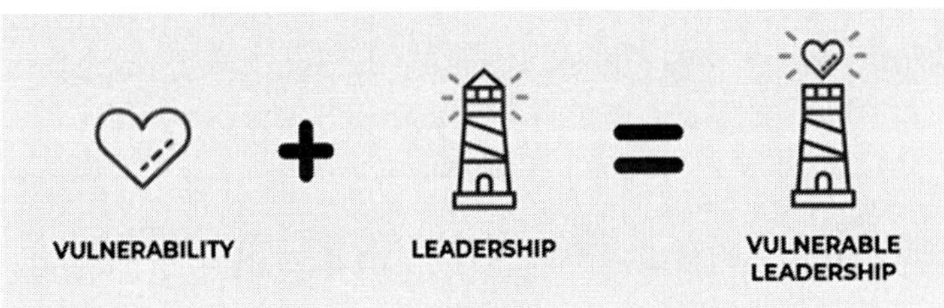


•••

## 5. Overcoming Leadership Challenges

There are some challenges (although they appear minor in the beginning, they can be major in the long run) especially when these challenges are about leaders, they not only impact themselves but also people around them and the overall outcomes. Some of the challenges are shared below:

1. One of the leaders felt very self-self-conscious introducing himself in a large gathering. He confessed that he suddenly felt conscious and that everyone was watching him!
2. In another instance, one of the leaders shared that he found it very difficult to express his thoughts in a meeting. Only when pushed, would he say yes/no and maybe a couple of words.
3. When one of his team members made a mistake, he would reprimand him severely, and later would regret that the message could have been given in a firm yet friendly manner.

In all the instances shared above, the focus of the challenge starts with the leader's self-esteem, background, and conditioning, and then is reflected in how it gets projected in the space of interpersonal relations. Everything is interconnected, and as a leader, the journey should start with the 'self'. The inside-out approach brings out the best results for the leader as well as for others. For the leader, the process requires willingness to dive deeper and take conscious and consistent steps to bring about a long-lasting change.

# B

# THE LEADER WITHIN

## 1. Managing time effectively

**Although I understand the need to be connected with my team members and update myself, I get pulled in day-to-day firefighting. How do I manage my time effectively?**

One of the most universal challenges seen especially in first-time managers and at times even seemingly experienced leaders, when they must walk the tightrope of getting work done from team members, connecting with them to understand ground realities, and keeping themselves updated too.

Managing time or must I say managing energy is a skill that all leaders should focus on cultivating at every stage. Some tools which they can follow to address this challenge.

1. Identifying your peak performance time during the day when you must do your deep work.
2. Using the Pomodoro technique **(The Pomodoro Technique — Why It Works & How to Do It (todoist.com))** for enhancing productivity.

3. Using the urgent-important matrix (**The Eisenhower Matrix: How to Prioritize Your To-Do List**) in prioritizing your day-to-day tasks.
4. Blocking your calendar every week/fortnight/month proactively to have your one-on-ones with team members.
5. Blocking your calendar every month/every quarter for updating/learning something new is a good practice.

**Which tools/techniques/frameworks are you using?**

•••

## 2. Avoiding Leadership Traps: Enhancing Effectiveness and Team Culture

Even the most experienced leaders can fall into common traps that hinder their effectiveness and impact their organizations negatively. From micromanagement to a lack of self-awareness, these traps can be subtle and insidious, creeping into leaders' behavior without their knowledge.

When people follow you blindly and consider you a demigod, you may be creating more yes-men/women around you!

1. **The Do-It-Myself Pit.** If you are jumping to solve all the problems on your table, then your team members will only rely on you for all the solutions. You need to move from telling them solutions to asking them the right questions, so that they start thinking and problem-solving.
2. **Falling victim to performance expectation extremes:** The extremes swing from tolerating mediocre results to creating an unsustainable pace where everything is a priority and nothing is ever good enough. Ask yourself where you fall on the expectation spectrum and adjust to the higher end without crossing into the hellish extreme.
3. **The Too-Busy-For-You Cage:** One of your most important tasks is managing your team. This not only means getting people to do their job but also giving them the opportunity to come to you with their concerns, questions, and opinions. Without your employees, your business is nothing. Show them that you value their contribution by being as available for them as possible. In addition to setting frequent meetings with them, ensure they have a channel where they can leave you messages and communicate with you directly.
4. **The So-Serious Snare:** You and your employees spend around a third of your waking hours at work, so make sure it's an enjoyable environment to be in. This could be small things such as an afternoon tea once in a while or celebrating big wins with a shared bottle of champagne. Whatever it is, be sure to show your workforce that you are a boss your employees can love, and their colleagues are people they can have fun with.
5. **The Lack-in-Communication Net:** It is vital that your workforce is constantly kept up to date with the

latest information about the business. Whether that's announcing a new hire, explaining why someone has left, or notifying about a systems change, ensure there is a clear channel for staff to learn about what's going on. Let your employees know that communication is a two-way street. Information fed to you through your employees could very well save your business.

In many cases, the leaders may not be aware, too, if they have fallen into any of the above traps. If you find yourself caught, make a conscious effort to change your behavior. If the working culture in your business isn't yet ideal, take a look in the mirror. Change usually needs to start at the top.

•••

## 3. From Good to Great: Key Pointers for Building Psychological Safety in Leadership

Leaders acknowledging their own fallibility, asking questions, and framing the task as a learning challenge – all these factors are essential to build psychological safety in the workplace. As a leader, if you are keen to up your game from 'Good to Great' in this space, check out some important markers:

### 1. REFRAME MISTAKES

***What good looks like:***

- Acknowledge that mistakes happen.
- Avoid showing anger when mistakes happen.
- Help team members correct mistakes.

***What great looks like:***

- Share your own mistakes vulnerably and often.
- Remind team members frequently that our work is complex and that we should expect mistakes.
- Reframe mistakes as steps in a longer journey, as valuable feedback and data we can work with, and as an opportunity to learn.

### 2. ENCOURAGE ALL VOICES

***What good looks like:***

- Every time there's a big decision, explicitly ask, *"Are we ready to move forward?"* and make sure everyone says *"yes."*
- Avoid using discrediting language when somebody shares (e.g., avoid saying things like "yes, but " or *"There is a lot of context that you don't know")*.

***What great looks like:***

- Actively avoid the "sunflower" effect, where others align with the view of the leader.
- Remind the team frequently of the power of having everyone share. Note that, in our complex world, leaders don't have all the answers and everyone has a unique and useful part of the answer. Ask people to share their thoughts as well as their feelings and underlying beliefs or assumptions.
- Invite participation in neutral, nonthreatening ways (e.g., "What could be a viewpoint we are missing? Are there any blind spots we missed?") and pause long enough for people to speak up.
- Set up formal team mechanisms to encourage sharing of ideas (e.g., have a standing "devil's advocate meeting" to pressure-test plans and ideas).
- Fill silences with questions instead of comments.
- Explain why certain points of view were not incorporated into a final decision; share the context and the decision-making process with the team transparently.

### 3. APPRECIATE CONTRIBUTIONS

***What good looks like:***

- Proactively and frequently acknowledge the good job that team members are doing.
- Say "thank you" when people speak up or go above and beyond the norm.

***What great looks like:***

- Make recognition part of your team's language and norms.
- Give special thanks to people who bring up uncomfortable, hard issues, recognizing contributions to the open group dynamic as much as problem solving.

- Be specific about any action that you celebrate and the impact it had on you.
- Acknowledge the points that others make during a meeting (e.g., "To build on Cara's point ...").

## 4. COACH TEAM MEMBERS TO HELP AND SUPPORT EACH OTHER

***What good looks like:***

- Encourage peer recognition (e.g., set a team norm to write a two-minute thank-you note every day).
- Remind team members that it is everyone's role to enhance the experience of others on the team.

***What great looks like:***

- Develop norms encouraging team members to give their views.
- Coach team members to support each other (e.g., ask them to ask deep questions to really understand what their team members are bringing to the discussion).
- Provide feedback and coaching to individual team members on their contributions to psychological safety.

•••

## 4. Until my manager yells at me, I don't realize that I have done something wrong!

This was the response I received when I was facilitating a workshop on 'Performance conversations' for a client recently. The focus of the conversation was on giving constructive feedback and asking the right questions to your team members. As we were discussing some of the techniques for giving constructive feedback and the importance of being mindful of the tone of voice while giving feedback, a participant just stood up and said, 'Until my manager yells at me, I don't understand and realize that I need to take action to change a behavior. If he gives me feedback without raising his voice, I don't feel the need to act.

This statement set us all thinking about the kind of conditioning our mind has about the way we are used to taking feedback. Most people prefer to have a firm yet friendly tone when receiving constructive feedback, a few may need to have a raised voice, which is only when they realize the need to act. The preference of each individual boils down to the kind of upbringing they had and the set of bosses they have experienced previously.

•••

# 5. The Power of Mindset in Leadership

Managers are told: Be global and be local. Collaborate and compete. Change, perpetually, and maintain order. Make the numbers while nurturing your people. To be effective, managers need to consider these juxtapositions in order to arrive at a deep integration of these seemingly contradictory concerns. That means they must focus not only on what they have to accomplish but also on how they have to think.

As managers, can we regularly check the mindsets we have in different workplace contexts?

Managing involves five tasks, each with its own mindset:

1. Managing the self *(the reflective mindset)*
2. Managing organizations *(the analytic mindset)*
3. Managing context *(the worldly mindset)*
4. Managing relationships *(the collaborative mindset)*
5. Managing change *(the action mindset)*

Each mindset overlaps with the others. However, in the autopilot mode in which we often operate, can we pause and reflect? Since mindset determines thoughts, thoughts determine actions, and actions determine results, it's valuable to check in daily for reflection, review, and change if needed. If not daily, can we dedicate time weekly to this introspection?

As a manager, how have you fared in different contexts? Do you need to make any changes?

**An inside-out approach always helps! What do you think?**

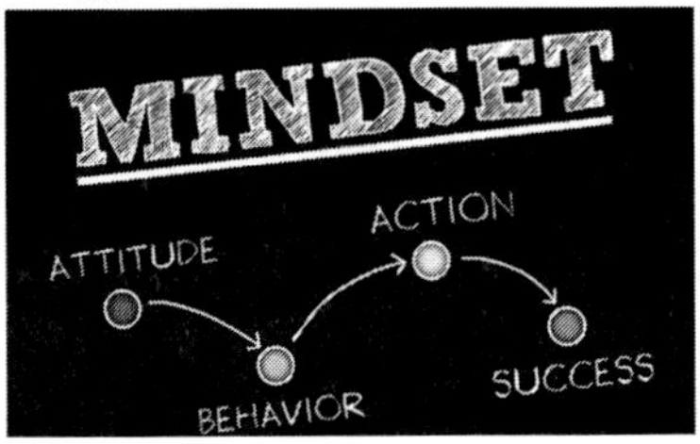

C

# EMOTIONAL COMPASS OF LEADERSHIP

## 1. Harnessing Passion for Growth

In my consulting experience, I have seen 'passion' manifest in different ways for individuals, teams, and organizations. It's absolutely amazing to see and experience this.

**At an individual level:**

1. Proactive behavior, trying to improve in one's area of expertise (because of commitment to domain), helping other team members to find their passion.
2. There is tremendous focus, clarity of thought, and high energy (one can see the 'spark' in one's eyes)
3. Many times, because of sharp focus, there is a lot of thinking that helps one see long-term plans as well.

**At a team level:**

1. Connecting, questing, finding common goals and relentlessly working towards them.
2. Open as many doors as possible.
3. Facilitate multistakeholder dialogue.
4. Embrace the positive side of collaboration tools.

5. The persistent attitude to focus on passion and not give up despite failures/obstacles along the way is important.
6. Consistently keep doing good without expecting results (read 'fruits') from the effort put in.

**At an organization level:**

1. Hire passionate people, let people show their emotions
2. **Fan the flames.** Find ways to share and celebrate the passion of your team. Augment your company newsletter by shooting videos of your people in action or find opportunities to throw culture-inspired parties to celebrate your joint accomplishments.
3. Give autonomy to people.
4. Create an environment to learn, grow, quest, and connect.

Of course, one may find 'passion' at different intensities in different companies.

**As a leader, what else are you doing to ignite the passion in your talent?**

•••

## 2. Are you noticing the signals?

We repeatedly ignore signals that function to keep our vehicle running. You probably ignore your basic needs for sleep, food, water, and going to the bathroom quite often. I have to admit, I do, because I regularly think that the work I'm doing at that moment is more important than refilling my water bottle.

- How often do you get a headache because you are dehydrated?
- Are you used to skipping meals because you don't have time to eat?
- And what about sleep? How often do you go to bed when you're feeling tired?
- How often do you take an afternoon nap because you feel you need it?

There's a high chance you're ignoring those signals frequently, heh? It sounds very childish, maybe, and it is so obvious that you should follow up on those basic signals. But sadly, a lot of us often don't do that.

But ignoring your body is the equivalent of slapping duct tape on your car's check engine light. How effective is that? In the short term, you may buy yourself some time, but the problem doesn't go away. And if you ignore it long enough, it's likely to result in a catastrophic physical breakdown. So, if you make the mistake of using your mind to override your body, you'll be highly productive—until you burn out or develop serious physical diseases. To arrive successfully at your destination, you need to pay attention to the internal condition of your vehicle while paying attention to the external driving conditions.

Likewise, I recently saw an organization where attrition was at its highest in two quarters. The triggers of this were seen and felt by leaders in earlier quarters; however, since the right actions were not taken at the right time, some of the good performers had left the organization. It was a very tricky situation, where the juniors were left orphaned, wondering what's coming up next for them, and the seniors were wondering how soon we can get new people in place.

**Just like our bodies, our people are also giving us signals. As leaders, are we listening, observing, and taking actions about them?**

•••

## 3. Recognizing and Developing Leadership Habits

At my first job, we had one manager who always said thank you to our team members. He'd recognize if one of us had to stay late, and he wouldn't miss the opportunity to thank us for our good work.

Those little thank-you messages meant a lot to me when I was nervous. They changed how I viewed my work. I'm sure I wasn't the only one who felt that way, either.

When people feel appreciated, it can change their outlook on work for the better.

But saying thank you to a team isn't as natural for some as it is for others. Here are some phrases which you can use and build on further:

- *I deeply appreciate every member of this team for showing relentless effort on this project.*
- *It gives me great pride to be the leader of this team. Your hard work continues to inspire me.*
- *I see and appreciate everything you do for the company.*
- *The success our organization has experienced would not be possible without your contribution.*
- *Thank you for remaining patient with me as I've adjusted to my managerial role. I appreciate your guidance and support.*
- *Fantastic job on meeting the deadlines. Your work ethic never ceases to amaze me.*

Trying to pick the right time and place might feel awkward too. We know it's a nice thing to say, and it's something we all want to get better at doing — but where do you begin?

- You've finished leading an extensive project and want to

congratulate the team on their success.

- Perhaps you want to thank your employees for trusting your leadership during a challenging period.
- One of your team members might be feeling down about himself or herself and your gratitude could lift them up again.
- Pick a time that ensures every member of your team receives your gratitude. It may be more impactful to show appreciation before your company closes for the holiday, which can spread your message while your employees are available.

**"What gets recognized, gets repeated!**

●●●

## 4. A Leader's Journey: From Novice to Expert

Performance = Potential – Interference

What can an individual do to identify and reduce/ eliminate his/her internal interruptions (mental blocks)?

The first step is to identify these internal interruptions (be it self-doubt, emotional block, or fear of looking incompetent) and then think of ways to manage them.

Some of the most common are:

**1. Emotional block**

Past experiences, traumas, or unresolved issues can create barriers (intense emotions like fear, anger, sadness) that get in the way of making decisions or solving problems.

**Example of an emotional block**

Imagine a seasoned executive named Sarah who's been in the business field for over a decade. Throughout her career, she's faced both challenges and achievements. But one particular experience has created an emotional block for her: an encounter with a toxic and manipulative manager.

In her previous role, Sarah worked tirelessly on a project. However, her manager, driven by personal ambition, consistently undermined her efforts and took credit for her work.

This experience left Sarah with a profound sense of betrayal, insecurity, and distrust in her professional relationships. She began doubting her abilities, second-guessing her ideas, and struggling to assert herself in meetings. This emotional block didn't allow her to take on leadership roles and limited her career progression.

**Questions to ask to address this mental block:**

1. What past experiences or traumas may have contributed to this emotional block?
2. Are there any patterns or triggers that activate this emotional block?
3. How can I challenge and reframe these beliefs or fears?

**2. Knowledge or skill gap block**

This block arises when you lack the necessary knowledge or skills to tackle a particular task or problem. It can make you feel stuck or unable to make progress because you're not equipped with the required information or abilities.

**Example of a knowledge or skill gap block**

Samantha is an entrepreneur who recently started her own e-commerce business. While she has a strong vision for her brand, she lacks the necessary skills to effectively promote her business online.

The knowledge or skill gap block significantly impacts Samantha and her business.

Firstly, she struggles to reach her target audience and navigate the complexities of online marketing channels. Moreover, she misses out on the chance to leverage social media platforms, search engine optimization, and targeted online advertising.

**Questions to ask to get over the mental block:**

1. What specific knowledge or skills do I need to acquire to overcome this block?
2. Can I turn to any specific courses, training programs or mentors to help me bridge this knowledge gap?

•••

## 5. Identifying Problematic Leadership Habits

Not everyone is a natural leader, and there is no guarantee that someone who lands in a leadership position will be a good leader. Many senior leaders and executives come into their roles with no formal leadership training or prior experience leading others. This can lead them to unconsciously develop negative habits that may demotivate their teams.

If leaders are able to recognize their problematic habits, they can work on changing them and become truly great leaders. Below, 16 members of Forbes Coaches Council share the most detrimental leadership habits they've observed in senior leaders and executives.Forbes Coaches Council

1. Overcommitting
2. Losing sight of broader goals
3. Discarding seemingly unlikely early warnings
4. Showing a lack of accountability
5. Lacking self-awareness
6. Not being curious about diverse talent in the team

7. Giving too much or not enough credit
8. Losing sight of the customer
9. Behaving in an inconsistent manner
10. Believing they know best.
11. Lacking empathy
12. Yelling, being late, and chewing gum.
13. Isolating themselves from their direct reports
14. Failing to assess employee needs and recalibrate.
15. Being prideful
16. Not understanding others' perspectives

**Do you see yourself demonstrating any of these qualities?**

•••

# D

# EMOTIONAL COMPASS OF LEADERSHIP

## 1. Potential vs. performance

When I was pursuing my graduation, choosing the major subject in the second year of graduation was like an approach-approach conflict for me. Two subjects had particularly stirred my interest— one was German, and the other one was Psychology. I had studied German in school; my scores were good (read performance) and hence had a natural inclination towards the subject. However, Psychology was a new subject for me and the way my teacher created interest in the subject was unparalleled. The idea that we can study how the mind works and its impact on our behavior was very intriguing to me as a student then. In addition, the various applications of Psychology in personal and professional life were a new insight for me. My teacher used the storytelling method to create interest in the subject and through these stories she used to nudge us to explore our own potential in the subject and start thinking about using our own strengths to convert the potential into performance. She had very gently sown the thought of looking beyond performance and focusing on utilizing one's potential.

Here is a question for leaders: How often do you go beyond the obvious act of looking at your team member's performance and nudge them to use their potential?

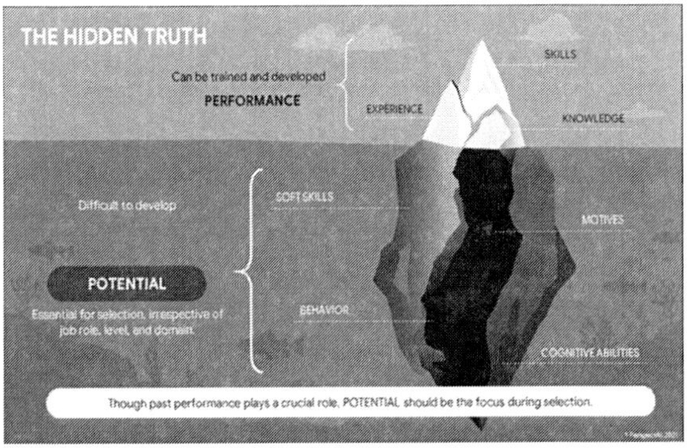


•••

## 2. How to avoid becoming an 'Absentee Leader?'

**Are you keen to identify Absentee Traits in yourself and How to Avoid Becoming an Absentee Leader. Here are some important steps:**

### 1. Self-Assessment

Regularly evaluating your own leadership style and behaviors is the first step in avoiding becoming an absentee leader. Utilize self-assessment tools and leadership surveys to gauge your effectiveness and identify any areas for improvement. This introspection can help you become more aware of any tendencies toward absentee behavior.

### 2. Feedback Loop

Creating an open environment where team members feel comfortable providing honest feedback is crucial. Actively seek out feedback from your team and take it seriously. This feedback loop can serve as an early warning system for any absentee tendencies and can guide you in making necessary adjustments to your leadership style.

### 3. Consult Peers

Peer consultation can offer valuable insights into your leadership style. Seek advice from other leaders within or outside your organization and compare leadership styles and strategies. This can provide you with a broader perspective and help you identify any potential shortcomings in your own approach.

### 4. Active Engagement

Make a conscious effort to be actively involved in your team's activities. This means not just being physically present but also participating in discussions, offering guidance, and providing constructive feedback. Active engagement can help you build a strong rapport with your team and ward off any tendencies toward absenteeism.

### 5. Regular Check-ins

Schedule regular one-on-one meetings with team members to discuss their progress, challenges, and any support they may need. These check-ins can serve as a platform for open communication and can help you stay engaged with your team's activities.

### 6. Constructive Feedback

Providing meaningful and constructive feedback is essential for the growth and development of your team. Make it a point to offer specific, actionable feedback that can help team members improve their performance. This not only aids in their professional development but also establishes you as an engaged and effective leader.

•••

## 3. How did my mentor help me to understand my strengths?

Early in my career, I had the opportunity to work with an HR consultant. Her focus areas were organization development and HR consulting. I gained amazing learning opportunities under her guidance—whether it was understanding concepts and frameworks in organization development or learning how they are applied in the corporate world to create the best people practices. From attention to detail, using the right words in the right context, understanding the importance of documentation, and navigating conversations in client meetings, every experience was a valuable learning opportunity for me.

After office hours, I used to teach Organization Behavior—a subject I loved— in an Executive MBA program. This gave me the chance to revisit books, prepare for my sessions, and interact with working professionals. After class, I would return to the office to pick up my things and have a quick chat with my boss about the day and how my session went.

She always noticed how energized I was after the classroom sessions, despite them being in the evening after office hours. In her words, "I always see you happy after you facilitate sessions for people." That was my validation in understanding my strength. I was fortunate to have a boss who encouraged me to sharpen my strengths both inside and outside the office.

Having a mentor in the workplace makes a world of difference, especially in the early years of one's career. It allows you to focus on and leverage your strengths with a learning mindset.

**What has been your experience?**

•••

# E

# THE LEADER'S LEGACY

## 1. Building a Leadership Brand

Whether you're aware of it or not, you already have a personal leadership brand. Everything you do or say (or don't do or say) communicates your identity as a leader to those around you.

How often – if ever – have you given thought to your leadership brand? Your leadership brand is, in essence, your personal brand. It's the total of your reputation and how you act, look, speak, think, and interact with others. The fact is, you have a leadership brand whether you like it or not – and it matters hugely to your professional career.

Here are four key things to bear in mind when building your leadership brand:

**1. Don't confuse your leadership brand with status.**

"As leaders we tend to define ourselves by what we do, by our social status, or by those around us." "Oh, I'm the CEO... I'm an engineer... I have two children... But that's not who you are." The danger with sharing status is that it "tends to come with comparison and judgment – said or unsaid."

Instead, by sharing their values and beliefs, leaders are more likely to be relatable to others and trusted by them.

**2. Base your brand on your passions**

"When you decide what to write about on LinkedIn, or speak about to the people you lead, find topics that you are really passionate about. Passion is so important when creating a leadership brand because it's contagious. It will enrol others in your brand. Don't focus on who's going to follow you or how what you say is going to land. Just focus on how what you're saying lands with you. It needs to be authentic, otherwise it will fall flat.

**3. Know your USP**

When assessing your unique selling point (USP), it is important to consider what your niche is. "Then think again of what your niche may be within that niche." Your brand story should be both interesting and memorable. It also helps to define a leader's purpose – which, put simply, is 'why do you exist?'"

It's important to remember that identifying your leadership brand is only the start of the journey. Once you have defined your personal brand, you need to live it every day. And that's when the hard work really begins.

**4. Offer value on social media**

One easy way to build your leadership brand is by offering your audience value-based content on social media. There is no such thing as giving too much value. The more you can share your values, beliefs, and experience with your followers, the more you will establish yourself as an authority figure and someone to be respected.

•••

# SECTION 2: CASE STUDIES

# A

# IDENTITY AND PRESENCE

## 1. Case Study: Building a personal brand

In a conversation with a young HR executive recently:

**Sara:** I want to build my personal brand on social media, and I am struggling in this space. Can you suggest ways in which I can build mine?

**Meeta:** I have benefited a lot from writing on LinkedIn consistently about my work and I can share some strategies that will help you to write consistently as well. Would you like to know more?

**Sara:** Sure, the idea is great; however, I feel, "What if I just get stuck in checking the number of likes and comments on my post?' I think I will just get stuck there. Hence, that can be a great distractor!

**Meeta:** And what if, even if you do, you will at least learn which posts are working well and how to take the writing journey further.

**Sara:** Hm…let me think!

Such "what if" thoughts pull us back in so many different contexts. They not only prohibit us from taking the initiative but also, in many cases, even when we are ready to take the first step, pull us back even further! Have you caught yourself in these instances and tried to break the loop?

**If you are a leader, what are the 'what if' thoughts that are pulling you back in connecting, developing, and inspiring team members?**

**Write your response:**

________________________________________

________________________________________

________________________________________

________________________________________

________________________________________

•••

## 2. Case study: Don't make modesty a virtue! It can be a roadblock when you are leading a team.

This was the feedback received by a leader from the top management in the context of leading a team. This leader, Siddharth, was responsible for leading a team of 20 people. He was a modest professional, and he would never beat his own drum and talk about his achievements. Likewise, he would become uncomfortable when someone would acknowledge his efforts or outcomes he had achieved. For him, this was a basic-level achievement that any person in his role should do, so why should someone take special notice and acknowledge it?

When it came to leading his team, although there were many forums where he could talk about his team with pride—their achievements, their growth—his modesty stopped him from doing so. Because of this, some of the team members felt that as a team they could never be in the limelight because the leader never spoke about it. When Siddharth got this feedback from the top management, he realized how modesty (generally considered a virtue) was becoming a roadblock when he was leading a team! Siddharth decided to take this feedback seriously and decided to work with a coach to consciously bring about a change in this area. The journey was not easy, but the decision to use the feedback seriously and work on it consciously itself was a great breakthrough. After working with his coach for five months, the team members started seeing the change in the way he was communicating and his body language too.

**Lessons Learned**

___________________________________________

___________________________________________

___________________________________________

___________________________________________

___________________________________________

•••

# B

# BIAS AND BLIND SPOTS

## 1. Case Study: Tackling Unconscious Bias

Have you ever uncovered your unconscious bias?

This is a story of my friend's daughter and her group of friends. I was visiting my friend last week and her daughter (11 years old) was busy playing with her friends outside the house. As I was about to leave, she brought her friends inside the house, and I casually asked one of the 'smart-looking' kids her name. When she shared her name, at the same time, I saw the kid right behind her (who was not-so-smart-looking) with an expression "why didn't she ask me my name?" I caught this "not-so-happy expression" on her face and it almost hit me really hard! Oh my god! while I did not intentionally ask the smart one her name, my bias crept in unknowingly and I did what I did!

On deeper reflection I realized that while we may take some actions unknowingly, our biases are directing our actions and thoughts. How often do we realise this?

**Likewise, a question here for leaders:**

You will have different team members because of their educational backgrounds, experiences, personality, culture, performance, etc. **Do you treat them differently?**

**Lessons Learned**

________________________________________

________________________________________

________________________________________

________________________________________

________________________________________

•••

## 2. Case Study: Identifying and Addressing Blind Spots

Blind spots can truly blind you if you don't seek feedback and work on them.

This is a story of a techie guy, Vishal (name changed), who along with a couple of friends started an organization a few years back. Each person had a completely different style of leading and managing people. Vishal came from a rough and tough background, the only way to get work done was to shout at people, and publicly criticizing them was very normal for him. He was a ruthless taskmaster! While he had the belief that he was open and honest, he was unaware that people were feeling disengaged in the process.

He was a strong technocrat, who believed that people were merely 'resources' to get work done. Initially, the team members were afraid of him, and they respected him as the leader - out of fear. His subtle arrogance could not be missed, especially by the old-timers in that company. The old-timers in the company had gotten used to his style of working. However, they used to feel bad when he used to publicly criticize someone. However, newer employees were not only surprised but shocked by his style of people management. Over a period of time, people started resigning - mentally and physically - because his leadership style was percolating down.

There was no one in the company who could offer this feedback to the leader and hence it became a huge blind spot for him. The company was bleeding—in terms of people resigning—when the HR team engaged me for a leadership coaching exercise. In this exercise, people started speaking up about his leadership style and how it was adversely impacting them. Micromanagement added fuel to his bad style of people management. I had to 'bell the cat'; I shared this feedback with Vishal and coached him the 'ask and listen approach' along with several coaching conversations to help him acknowledge and take ownership of his blind spots.

It took a few months with this leader to drop his resistance, confront his blind spots and work through them for his own and the organization's benefit. Once he embraced this transformation, the needle began to move in the right direction.

Once blind spots are identified, especially of leaders, the right action to address them should be started as soon as possible; otherwise, it can be a big derailer for the organization.

**Lessons Learned**

________________________________________

________________________________________

________________________________________

________________________________________

________________________________________

•••

# C

# ORGANIZATIONAL LEADERSHIP GAPS

## 1. Case Study: Absentee Leadership in Companies

Several high-profile companies have experienced the negative impacts of absent leadership:

**Uber:** During the tenure of then-CEO Travis Kalanick, Uber faced numerous controversies, ranging from allegations of sexual harassment to a toxic work culture. Kalanick's leadership style was often criticized for being detached from the day-to-day operations and employee wellbeing, leading to significant reputational and internal strife.

**General Electric (GE):** During the tenure of Jeff Immelt as CEO, General Electric faced several strategic missteps attributed to absent leadership. Immelt was often criticized for being disconnected from the company's operational realities and failing to anticipate market shifts. This led to poor strategic decisions such as overinvestment in fossil fuels and underinvestment in renewable energy. These missteps culminated in a sharp decline in GE's stock value and necessitated major restructuring.

**Boeing:** Boeing's 737 Max crisis highlighted severe leadership failings. The company's leadership was criticized for being disconnected from critical operational and safety matters. Former CEO Dennis Muilenburg's handling of the crisis was seen as inadequate, marked by a lack of transparency and accountability. This absence of engaged leadership led to significant safety concerns, grounding of the aircraft, financial losses, and a damaged reputation.

**What lessons can we learn from these examples?**

___

___

___

___

___

•••

## 2. Case Study: The Power of Realistic Leadership Insights

**Start-up leader:** I am keen to groom a few of my team members into a leadership role, as I intend to scale up the organization

**Meeta:** Sure, could you please share the SWOT exercise that you have done with them.

**Start-up leader:** Sure, here it is! According to me A, D, E, and F seem ready to take on new responsibilities.

**Meeta:** (After having three coaching conversations with each of them) From my conversations with them, I feel that they are capable as 'senior functionaries' (they can grow more as technical experts than leaders)

**Start-up Leader:** Wow, Meeta! This is an amazing insight for me and many thanks for sharing this, because over the last few years, since I have been closely working with the team, I was emotionally attached to them and had an idealized perspective about their skills and willingness to become leaders. Your observation helps me gain a realistic perspective, and I can now modify my approach based on this perspective.

Leadership is an everyday journey, and it's very easy to become emotionally attached to your team members over time. A coach can help you gain a realistic perspective of the context and bring out the best in your team.

**Lessons Learned**

_______________________________________________

_______________________________________________

_______________________________________________

_______________________________________________

_______________________________________________

•••

# D

# SHAPING MINDSETS

## 1. Case Study: Reflecting on Your Mindset

In a recent conversation with one of my coaches, she mentioned that she has been working in the current organization for almost 7 years and has been exposed to several functions—right from Accounts, Purchase, to Digital Marketing. Besides understanding the nuances in different functions, she recalled that every time she has been delivering outcomes, it has come from a place of 'fear' (since her boss is a perfectionist and demands work completed to the 'T'; if that does not happen, there would be a consequence) Over a period of time, while she was learning, she realized that operating from a fearful mindset was creating more errors and mistakes in her outcomes. This realization helped her change her mindset to one of ownership and look at work outcomes from the perspective of giving her best and focusing on 'excellence' rather than just submitting something out of fear. This shift in mindset, not only elevated her confidence, but the ownership mindset also helped her boss give her more responsibilities too.

**Have you had a reflective conversation recently? What was your experience?**

___

___

___

___

___

•••

# SECTION 3: ACTIVITY

# MANAGERIAL PERSONALITY TEST

**Instructions:**

- Answer the following questions honestly based on your natural tendencies at work.
- Choose the option that best represents your usual behaviour.
- At the end, add up your scores to discover your managerial personality type.

**1. How do you handle delegation?**

a. I trust my team and delegate tasks with minimal supervision.

b. I delegate but often check in to ensure things are on track.

c. I prefer to handle important tasks myself to ensure quality.

d. I find it hard to let go and usually end up doing everything myself.

**2. How do you handle conflict in your team?**

a. I address it directly and mediate to find a fair solution.

b. I prefer to let people resolve conflicts themselves unless it escalates.

c. I avoid conflicts and hope they resolve over time.

d. I find conflicts stressful and tend to take sides.

**3. How do you motivate your team?**

a. By setting clear goals and empowering them.

b. By offering encouragement and appreciation.

c. By setting strict rules and deadlines.

d. I assume people should motivate themselves.

**4. How do you handle underperformance in your team?**

a. Provide constructive feedback and support their development.

b. Give them time and guidance to improve.

c. Confront them directly and demand improvement.

d. Ignore it and hope it improves on its own.

**5. What's your approach to decision-making?**

a. I involve my team and encourage collaboration.

b. I take input from others but make the final call.

c. I make decisions quickly without much discussion.

d. I struggle to make decisions and often delay them.

**6. How do you handle feedback from your team?**

a. I welcome it and encourage open communication.

b. I consider it but don't always act on it.

c. I feel uncomfortable when receiving feedback.

d. I dismiss criticism and prefer to lead without input.

**7. How do you manage stress?**

a. I stay calm, prioritize tasks, and delegate effectively.

b. I manage stress by talking to my team and problem-solving together.

c. I tend to get overwhelmed but push through.

d. I frequently feel burned out and exhausted.

**8. What best describes your leadership style?**

a. Supportive and empowering.

b. Collaborative and engaging.

c. Directive and results-driven.

d. Detached and uninvolved.

Count how many times you choose each letter (A, B, C, or D)

| Options | Times Selected |
|---|---|
| A | |
| B | |
| C | |
| D | |

**Your leadership type is determined by the letter you selected most often.**

**A – The Transformational Leader**

You inspire and empower your team, focus on their development, and build a positive workplace culture. People look up to you for guidance and vision.

**B – The Collaborative Manager**

You value teamwork and encourage input from your team. You balance results with employee well-being and foster a cooperative work environment.

**C – The Task-Oriented Manager**

You focus on efficiency and results, but you may need to improve team motivation and communication. Improving delegation and engagement can enhance your leadership.

**D – The Overwhelmed Manager**

You may struggle with delegation, communication, or managing stress. Developing leadership skills, learning to delegate, and encouraging open communication can help you improve.

**Next Steps:**

- Reflect on your score.
- What are your strengths and areas for improvement?
- Decide what specific changes you can make to enhance your leadership.

•••

# PART 3
# ORGANIZATIONAL CULTURE AND EMPLOYEE ENGAGEMENT

# INDEX

# SECTION 1: CHAPTERS

# A

# LEADERSHIP AND CULTURE BUILDING

## 1. Leadership's Role in Shaping Organizational Culture

Culture is a collection of beliefs, actions, and behaviors that are encouraged and tolerated within an organization.

Our experience tells us that organizations may have great policies. However, everyday experience is largely in the hands of immediate managers. Organizational culture refers to a system of shared meaning held by members that distinguishes one organization from another. This system of shared meaning is a set of key characteristics that the organization values. Research suggests that there are seven primary characteristics that in the aggregate capture the essence of an organizational culture.

1. **Innovation and risk-taking—** The degree to which employees are encouraged to be innovative and take risks.
2. **Attention to detail:** The degree to which employees are expected to exhibit precision, analysis, and attention to detail.

3. **Outcome orientation:** The degree to which management focuses on results or outcomes rather than on techniques or processes used to achieve these outcomes.
4. **People orientation:** The degree to which management decisions take into consideration the effect of outcomes on people within the organization.
5. **Team orientation:** The degree to which work activities are organized around teams rather than individuals.
6. **Aggressiveness:** The degree to which people are aggressive and competitive rather than easy-going.
7. **Stability:** The degree to which organizational activities emphasize maintaining the status quo in contrast to growth.

**As a leader, which behaviors are you encouraging and tolerating?**

•••

## 2. A Manager's Outlook

In a client meeting recently, one of the challenges they shared was that some of their managers had become mere 'postmen'. They have become so transactional (postman-like) in their communication with their team members that they just share the client's requirement with their team (having little or no knowledge about it!) to get the work done.

The reason for this is the huge churn of talent; managers tend to spend very little time understanding the length and breadth of their role; hence, their competence level is considerably basic or low, thereby impacting their self-confidence too! This has an impact on the culture of the team and finally that of the organization too!

On the other hand, I met a set of managers with another client, who were very keen to understand, learn, and grow in the length and breadth of their roles! (In short, their learning appetite was remarkably high compared to the earlier example). This helped them to be not only competent but also confident in their current roles and their future prospects.

Another differentiator between both examples was also the urban background of the managers in the first example – where the focus is more on salary, status, and infrastructure, etc. offered by the organization. Whereas, managers in the second example were from a Tier 2 city, where their primary focus was to learn and grow by remaining with the organization.

A manager's behavior has a great impact on employee engagement and, in turn, sets the tone for the organizational culture too.

•••

## 3. Attitude: The Precursor to Outcomes

Attitude Precedes Outcome

"We want solutions, but what we really need are attitudes. You don't need abs, but rather an attitude of training. You don't need the answer, but rather an attitude of curiosity. You don't need an easier life, but rather an attitude of perseverance.

"Attitude precedes outcome."

You don't need a policy to appreciate people; you need an attitude to recognize them.

This thought came to me during a discussion with a cohort of cross-functional stakeholders in a client organization.

The topic was: Should the HR Manager be responsible for informing all Functional Heads about identifying the 'Employee of the Month'?

**Whose Responsibility Is It?**

Instead of relying solely on an HR-driven policy, why not create a culture of appreciation where managers naturally recognize their team members' contributions?

While the HR Manager can facilitate the process, what stops immediate managers from appreciating their team members in different scenarios?

**Recognition vs. Appreciation**

- Recognition is about giving positive feedback based on results or performance. It can be an award, a bonus, or a promotion.
- Appreciation is about acknowledging a person's inherent value. It helps build trust and connection.

Recognition is about what people do, while appreciation is about who they are.

When leaders and managers take conscious steps to build trust, connection, and a culture of recognition and appreciation, a positive work environment becomes an obvious outcome.

•••

## 4. The Role of Humor in Leadership

Research shows that leaders with a sense of humour are seen as 27% more motivating and admired than those who don't joke around. Their employees are 15% more engaged and their teams are more than twice as likely to solve a creativity challenge, all of which can translate into improved performance.

Humour works as a social lubricant to build and sustain harmonious relationships. It is a much better way to raise sensitive issues. It is accepted as a socially appropriate means to express aggressive feelings or negative emotions. It helps give a very subtle message. Humour is also a way to break through the hierarchy. It's a great icebreaker and removes the walls that exist between leaders and followers. When an employee asks his manager, "Do you have a minute?" and the manager says, "No, I have 60 seconds," you are likely to be comfortable reaching out to such a manager.

Humour is not always good. Martin has classified humour into 4 types:

1. **Affiliative:** Affiliative humour is used to enhance one's relationships with others in a way that is relatively benign and self-accepting.
2. **Self-enhancing:** Self-enhancing humour is used to enhance the self in a way that is tolerant and non-detrimental to others.
3. **Aggressive:** Users of aggressive humour typically have little regard for the feelings of the targets of their humour; they are more concerned with getting a laugh and feeling superior.
4. **Self-defeating:** Self-defeating humour involves excessively disparaging humour or attempts to ingratiate oneself

or gain the approval of others by doing or saying funny things at one's expense.

These affiliative and self-enhancing styles are considered to be positive while aggressive and self-defeating are considered to be negative. One should make sure to choose humor appropriately.

Some of the most respected corporations have created fun workplace environments. Zappos, Warby Parker, Southwest Airlines, Chevron and Google have made their mark by creating a culture of fun. These companies have used humour and a positive, fun culture to help brand their business, attract and retain employees, and attract customers.

**As a leader or an organization do you encourage humor at the workplace? What has been your experience?**

•••

# B

# TRUST, RECOGNITION & ENGAGEMENT

## 1. The LEAP Framework for Team Recognition

The research is clear: gratitude is beneficial for you, the person you're thanking, and your team. But how should you express gratitude at work? How can you thank your colleagues in a meaningful way?

Here is an interesting framework that can help managers and leaders express appreciation effectively. It is called the L-E-A-P Framework:

**L - Learning**

Acknowledge any new learning a team member has had recently—be it a certification, training, webinar, accreditation, course completion, or on-the-job learning. Appreciate their effort in gaining new knowledge, encourage them to apply it in real time, and support them as they share their journey ahead.

**E - Efforts**

Often, the efforts a team member puts in are either taken for granted or only recognized when results are achieved.

However, appreciating their hard work—regardless of the outcome—can boost morale. Recognizing their dedication also allows you to guide them with smart strategies to achieve results more effectively.

**A - Achievements**

Celebrate achievements, big or small. Whether it's turning around a difficult customer, achieving targets early, enhancing product quality, saving costs, or any other milestone, acknowledging these successes encourages team members to strive for more. Regular celebrations of wins foster motivation and growth.

**P - People**

For new team members, onboarding should include a warm welcome and proper introductions to ease their integration into the team. Existing team members should also be celebrated for their contributions. Recognizing them as valuable individuals rather than just "resources" makes them feel valued and engaged.

**Why Recognition Matters**

Recognizing your team members is not just a nice thing to do—it's a smart thing to do. It helps build trust, engagement, and collaboration, while also improving productivity, quality, and job satisfaction.

By following the L-E-A-P Framework, you can appreciate your team members in a way that is meaningful, relevant, and impactful—both for them and for your organization.

## 2. Empowering Teams for Success

Are you a leader who wants to give opportunities to team members struggling with certain skills, allow them to make mistakes, or encourage them to try something new? When leaders take such steps, they create a psychologically safe environment for their team.

Psychological safety is about creating a workplace where employees feel safe to be themselves, speak up, and share their ideas without fear of being judged, ostracized, or punished.

The benefits of psychological safety are numerous, including:

1. **Improved Employee Engagement**

When employees feel safe sharing their opinions, they are more likely to engage in discussions, take ownership of their work, and feel a sense of purpose in their roles. This leads to increased productivity and job satisfaction.

2. **Enhanced Creativity and Innovation**

A psychologically safe environment encourages employees to express their ideas freely. This fosters creativity, innovation, and problem-solving, as employees are more willing to take risks and explore new approaches.

3. **Higher Retention Rates**

Employees who feel valued and appreciated in a psychologically safe environment are more likely to stay with the company long-term. This reduces turnover and enhances team stability.

4. **Increased Trust and Respect**

When employees feel they can be themselves and share their thoughts openly, it fosters mutual trust and respect between employees and leadership. This strengthens team cohesion and collaboration.

**Creating psychological safety in the workplace isn't just a leadership trend—it's a powerful strategy for building a high-performing, engaged, and innovative team.**

•••

## 3. Building trust in teams

Recently, in a meeting with an MD of an organization, he mentioned that his teams don't work collaboratively for the first 9 months of the year and suddenly in the last 3 months they seem to drop their egos and move towards achieving the targets!

When I heard this statement, I was stunned!

When there is a lack of trust within teams, people get into siloed working and would conveniently hold on to their egos and keep them aside when pressure mounts towards the end of the year!

When building and maintaining trust within a team, it is important to recognize that there are different levels of trust. Obviously, this isn't a definitive list, but the levels can largely be broken down into three distinct categories:

1. **Foundational**: On the most basic level, there is an expectation that team members can be relied upon to do their part and keep any promises or agreements they have made.
2. **Established**: At the next level, there is the understanding that each member has the best interests of the team at heart and can be trusted to act with integrity.
3. **Vulnerable**: Finally, there is a level of trust in which each member knows that they can rely on one another for support as well as professional guidance.

As a leader, one needs to know the level of trust that team members are demonstrating and take consistent actions to build trust within the team.

Here are some ways to build trust within teams:

- Set expectations and boundaries
- Create a space for psychological safety
- Demonstrate transparency.
- Conduct team-building activities
- Hold regular one-on-one meetings to check in
- Communicate effectively
- Be the first to admit when you're wrong
- Show appreciation for each team member's contribution
- Celebrate milestones together
- Lead by example

**Trust is like oxygen! When it is not there, it will hit you hard! Hence, building a transparent culture is a day-to-day exercise.**

•••

## 4. Enhancing the 'Approachability quotient of managers'

We hear this phrase – '**approachability quotient**' being used very often by managers and leaders across organizations. But how does one really practice this? Some managers I have worked with have demonstrated this through their practices consistently over a period of time. Sharing a couple of them:

1. **'Listening Diaries':** This is a practice of a supervisor who used to spend time sitting on the shop floor every Friday from 10 a.m. to 3 p.m. and he used to diligently take notes in his diary while he was listening to people. This practice was called 'Listening Diaries' because taking notes helped him remember details while he sat on the shop floor listening to the challenges and concerns of his team members. When the team members used to see their supervisor practice this every week, the amount of connection and quality of connect increased, which also helped build trust.
2. **'I am All Ears':** As the Chief People Officer (CPO) of a software organization with 30,000 employees spread across 6 countries in four to five different time zones, this CPO designed a practice called – 'I am All Ears'. His purpose was to block his calendar every Tuesday and Friday for one hour 5:30 to 6:30 IST and listen to the challenges and concerns of different stakeholders across the globe. By making himself available, he not only demonstrated his keenness to listen to their grievances but also showed that he was approachable despite the time and distance.

An action can be episodic; however, a practice is a consistent and conscious action done over a period of time.

**As managers, would you like to raise your game by designing and implementing such practices?**

•••

# C

# LEADERSHIP PRACTICES & CHALLENGES

## 1. Best Practices for Effective Leadership

"I have been putting all my efforts into my team members to keep them satisfied, but despite this, they resign and leave. I feel frustrated because the moment I feel they are almost ready for a critical project, they put in their resignation. I feel frustrated and helpless!

Deepak was sharing this experience while attending my leadership workshop recently. In my experience there are very few leaders who focus on truly connecting, developing, and inspiring their team members consistently. Here are 6 secrets to create a great sense of belongingness and strengthening their trust so that they choose to contribute and grow with you.

1. **Make work-life balance a priority:** A leader I have known has created a practice where he leaves the office on time and does not celebrate people who stay late. He also is a fitness freak, so he role models this behavior and encourages others to follow too.
2. **Make employees part of the big picture:** Benefits such as clear and frequent communication on company

happenings, individual and departmental direction, and big-picture company direction make all the difference in employee happiness.

3. **Be transparent and honest.** After a recent companywide engagement survey, we chose to share our results with all employees. We not only communicated our top areas of success but also our areas for improvement and how we planned to address them moving forward. Transparent communication and a simple acknowledgment that we heard them can go a long way.
4. **Create career pathways.** Planning career conversations at least once a quarter not only helps them to bridge the gap between their aspirations and abilities but also creates a sense of belonging.
5. **Recognition and Appreciation.** Employee recognition can be attained in a variety of ways, and team leaders have the opportunity to lean on their creative side. Peer-to-peer recognition programs, value-based recognition (identifying value champions), team outings and get-togethers, personalized thank-you notes and recognition boards are effective practices. Timely appreciation goes a long way in not only boosting the self-esteem of the individual but also encouraging him/her to repeat that behavior.
6. **Offer benefits beyond the basics.** "There are many ways to supplement salary by assisting employees in other areas of their lives. You can offer an extra level of life insurance or disability insurance for employees to protect their incomes. Other ancillary benefits, such as dental, optical and wellness, are all well received by employees. And gym memberships and transit benefits are great perks to keep employees happy and healthy. It is important to provide

higher benefits, so your employees know that you truly care about them and their families."

•••

## 2. Managing internal stakeholders

**Are decisions taking too long and slowing down work?**

Knowing who your internal stakeholders are and how to work with them can help you avoid these problems. But who exactly are internal stakeholders? Why are they important? And how do you influence them?

Internal stakeholders come from within a business or project team.

Most of the time they have a direct interest in a project's success because they typically rely on the results of the goals or projects for their own gain.

The role internal stakeholders play within a project or in a business also directly translates into project performance. This influence can be due to their roles in the organization, their daily activities (work), or long-term strategic commitments.

For most, influencing externally comes more easily, but when you have to influence internally, there is a mountain of factors and intricacies to navigate.

- Understand their role in the organization and project and the influence they can have on the outcomes
- Create opportunities to emphasize your decision-making powers
- Be proactive: point out the things that are most important to them
- Find common interests
- Pinpoint your 'must-wins'

**What other methods/techniques have you used to influence internal stakeholders?**

•••

## 11. Managing employee exits effectively

Meera (name changed) was working with Zesty Consulting for the last five years as a Program Manager. The company was not doing well in terms of business, and they were asking some people to leave the organization. Unfortunately, Meera was going to be one of them! The CEO, however, shared this news with Meera by just saying that she would not receive her salary from next month. When Meera heard this, she was dumbfounded and became emotional since she had least expected this news. Also, the way this was shared with her, she didn't like it at all. She went into the denial phase and continued going to the office for three months after this episode, too (of course, without getting paid!). She couldn't digest the fact that she was asked to leave and that she would have to look for a new job eventually. After the three months were over, she swallowed the hard reality and stopped going to the office. She accepted and decided to face the 'reality as it is'.

Organizational systems are powerful and complex and are full of tensions, dynamics, hidden fears and loyalties. Leaving brings up a lot of emotions for people, both those who are leaving and those who are being left. There are many, many circumstances associated with difficult leavings, but no matter what leads to the leaving, it can still be achieved with a mutual respect for what has been exchanged. This includes a respect for the person at an individual level, a respect for the wider system needs, and a respect for the truth around the reasons for departure. In most cases, it's important to really acknowledge what the person who is leaving has contributed. Even in circumstances when their contribution was limited or compromised, it's important to publicly thank them for what they were able to contribute, whilst also acknowledging that what they did was not enough in other areas.

**As an employer/as a HR Manager, what are the practices which you follow during employee exits that don't leave a bitter taste for both sides?**

•••

## 3. Building an accountability culture

As great people managers, how can we encourage people to take ownership at the workplace?

1. Creating psychologically safe spaces where people feel comfortable making mistakes, sharing new experiences, and asking questions is essential.

**'Goof-up'** is a practice started by a manager once every month where he shares the mistakes he made and the lessons learned from them. This builds openness and trust for the team members to share their own mistakes. It is a very powerful practice to own up to mistakes and, more importantly, share lessons learned so that mistakes are not repeated.

2. Ownership also comes in when they believe in their skills and their manager supports them in building those skills. This encourages a learning culture so that team members

will believe in their skills and their manager will support them in developing them.

**'Parikrama'** is a practice started by a manager who sets learning goals for himself and also encourages team members to do likewise. Every fortnight they share the learning progress with one another. The literal meaning of the word 'Parikrama' is 'completing a circle,' and this is what the practice is about (starting with self, involving, and encouraging others in their learning journey, and concluding with self. It's a learning 'accountability circle' of sorts.)

3. Involving and nurturing team members by giving them opportunities can help them take accountability in different contexts.

**Aj ka Don-** The objective of this practice is to develop team members for higher roles. The manager selects one team member every week to join the daily planning meeting. They are encouraged to interact in the meeting. This provides the team members exposure to the discussions happening in the meeting and allows them to interact with the seniors, giving them a meaningful, enriching, and memorable experience. Further, it improves their visibility among seniors too.

Sharing lessons learned, encouraging learning and development opportunities, and involving team members in different contexts are some of the best practices to create an 'accountability culture'.

## 4. Maximizing the Impact of Stretch Goals

### Can a stretch goal be ineffective?

A stretch goal is an ambitious objective that requires high effort and carries a level of risk. It is intentionally set above normal standards to drive growth, identify new opportunities, and gain valuable experience. By setting stretch goals, employers can help their employees break free from complacency and strive for high performance.

A stretch goal can become ineffective if the leader/manager demonstrates any one or more of the following behaviours:

1. When the goal is an 'instructive directive' (with non-involvement of the team in the goal-setting process) he/she can set unrealistic goals, which can lead to non-engagement of team members and eventually to burnout.
2. Not breaking down larger goals into smaller chunks gives team members the feeling that the goal is too vague and hence unachievable. They may not get a 'sense of direction' and hence can feel disengaged.
3. When the leader doesn't encourage and support team members to acquire new skills, knowledge, tools, and techniques, they can feel ill-equipped to move ahead in the goal achievement process, and hence may get stuck and disengaged.
4. A stretch goal is not meant to be a mandatory achievement; failure is a natural part of the process. The team members can feel discouraged if the leader doesn't support them in embracing failure as an opportunity to learn and grow.

Involving team members in the goal-setting process, breaking down larger goals into smaller chunks, supporting and encouraging team members to learn new skills, tools, and techniques, providing the necessary resources required, embracing failure as a learning opportunity, and encouraging the team to move forward, can help the individuals and teams to unleash their true potential!

•••

# D

# LEARNING, GROWTH & PERFORMANCE

## 1. Tracking Training Effectiveness

Only 12% of employees apply new skills learned in L&D programs to their jobs (HBR).

Are you confident that your Learning and Development initiatives are part of that 12%? And do you have the data to back it up?

L&D professionals who can track the business results of their programs report higher satisfaction with their services, more executive support, and continued and increased resources for L&D investments.

Learning is always specific to each employee and requires personal context. Evaluating training effectiveness shows you how useful your current training offerings are and how you can improve them in the future. What's more, effective training leads to higher employee performance and satisfaction, boosts team morale, and increases your return on investment (ROI). As a business, you're investing valuable resources in your training programs, so it's imperative that you regularly identify what's working, what's not, why, and how to keep improving.

To identify the right employee training metrics for your training program, here are a few important pointers:

Consult with key stakeholders – before development – on the metrics they care about. Make sure to use your L&D expertise to inform your collaboration.

Avoid using L&D jargon when collaborating with stakeholders – Modify your language to suit the audience.

Determine the value of measuring the effectiveness of a training program. It takes effort to evaluate training effectiveness, and those that support key strategic outcomes should be the focus of your training metrics.

Avoid highlighting low-level metrics, such as enrollment and completion rates.

•••

## 2. Addressing Root Causes in Leadership Development: Beyond the Symptoms

Are you addressing the symptoms, or do you want to address the root cause issue?

In a workshop that I facilitated recently for one of my clients, the questions participants asked and the challenges that they posed were around the following themes:

- How to address the bad attitude of internal stakeholders?
- How to stop the blame and defensive culture?
- How to work effectively with different generations?
- How can we create a collaborative culture?
- How to move from a victim mindset to a solution-focused mindset?

While the workshop did address the challenges and helped the participants to understand the different tools and frameworks to bring about a positive change, it would be impactful in the short term only. In the long term, the symptoms would again crop up, and the culture would re-emerge!

A question to CHROs and L & D professionals— Are you addressing the root cause of the issue or just the symptoms?

•••

## 3. How can a leader help team members enhance their performance?

**How Leaders Can Help Team Members Move from 'Meets Expectations' to 'Exceeds Expectations'**

Flexing your leadership style based on a team member's skill and will can significantly impact their performance. Here are a few key strategies leaders can use to elevate their team's performance:

**1. Set Clear Expectations**

Clearly communicate your expectations and set stretch goals to encourage team members to push beyond their comfort zones. This clarity helps them understand what they need to do to exceed expectations and tap into their full potential.

**2. Provide Regular Feedback**

Offer consistent and constructive feedback to help your team members identify strengths and areas for improvement. Providing feedback in a way that empowers and encourages them ensures they remain motivated to enhance their performance.

**3. Encourage Creativity**

Create a safe space for team members to think creatively and experiment with new ideas. Encouraging innovation helps employees move beyond routine tasks and actively contribute to organizational growth.

**4. Recognize Good Work**

Acknowledge and reward employees who exceed expectations in a timely and meaningful manner. Recognition reinforces positive behavior and motivates others to strive for excellence.

## 5. Provide Opportunities for Growth

Offer customized learning opportunities such as self-paced courses, online learning, coaching, mentoring, and hybrid training programs. Encouraging employees to apply newly acquired skills and tracking their progress fosters a culture of continuous learning and improvement.

## 6. Lead by Example

Demonstrate excellence in your own work to set a high standard for your team. When leaders consistently exceed expectations, they inspire their teams to follow suit.

Helping team members transition from "meets expectations" to "exceeds expectations" requires patience, dedication, and an investment in their growth and development. By implementing these strategies, you can empower your team to reach their full potential and drive organizational success.

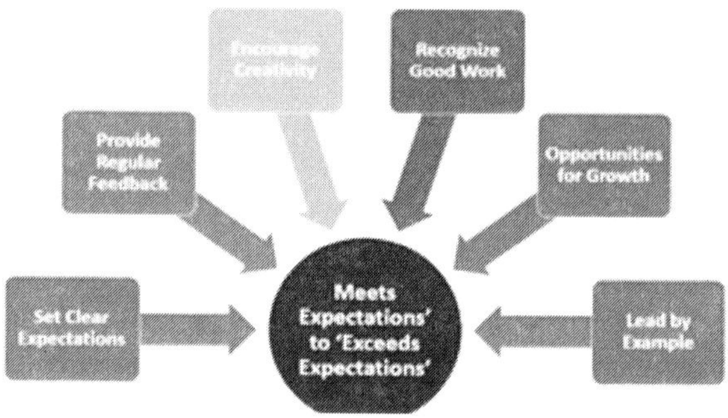


•••

# 4. Best Practices in Organizational Learning and Development

The best L&D practices are centered around aligning learning initiatives with business goals, ensuring continuous reskilling and upskilling, and measuring the effectiveness of L&D programs. Here are some best practices I have seem some organizations I have partnered with:

1. Leaders' role-modeling a learning culture—by learning something new or upskilling themselves consistently thereby inspiring others around them.
2. Involving leadership team and Business Unit Heads in identifying the learning objectives and outcomes
3. Being a proactive partner by aligning learning objectives with organizational goals.
4. Seeking inputs on participants' real-time challenges by conducting focused group discussion with a representative sample of the participants so that participants feel involved right from the design stage.
5. Participants take ownership of attending and participating fully in the learning interventions ( without HR or L&D follow-ups)
6. L &D teams conducting post-training reviews and adopting the 70-20-10 learning model to sustain and embed the learning culture
7. Harnessing the power of technology
8. Design learning to be embedded into the workflow.
9. Use granular, bite-sized, chunked learning methods.
10. Personalize training and make it flexible.
11. Establish metrics and dashboards to track learning impact and business outcomes.

12. Create cross-functional learning communities to encourage peer learning and collaboration.
13. Recognize and celebrate continuous learners to reinforce a growth mindset.
14. Integrate coaching and mentoring into post-learning reinforcement plans.

Which other best practices do you know that can be added to this list?

•••

## 5. Mastering the Art of Asking Questions: A Key Leadership Skill

Although there isn't one single trait that makes an effective leader, one common skill shared among them is mastery of the art of asking questions.

When you get into a regular cadence of asking your people the right one-on-one questions, it allows you to:

- Proactively uncover issues before they manifest
- Help employees grow and develop at a quicker rate
- Get to the heart of what's most important in every conversation, especially during 1-on-1s

This practice will also help enhance the employee experience in different conversations. To enhance employee experience, every leader should seek answers to these three questions:

**1. What are his/her strengths?**

Scheduling one-on-ones with your team members is a great opportunity to understand their strengths beyond formal processes like performance appraisals, 360-degree feedback, etc.

**2. What are the triggers that activate those strengths?**

To leverage your team member's strengths, a leader must make an effort to understand what activates those strengths. Some triggers could be:

- A specific time of the day
- Time with leaders
- Autonomy in work
- Addressing challenges
- Recognition (public praise, one-on-one feedback, customer appreciation, awards, or letters from stakeholders)
- Customizing recognition methods according to individual preferences can be a game-changer.

**3. What is his/her learning style?**

People have different learning preferences in the workplace. Understanding these styles helps leaders communicate more effectively—especially during training or performance improvement.

The four basic learning styles:

- Visual learners - prefer graphics and videos
- Auditory learners - learn best through listening
- Reading-focused learners - excel with text-based materials
- Kinesthetic learners - prefer hands-on experiences

**How to identify learning styles?**

Visual learners ask, "Can you demonstrate that for me?"

Auditory learners ask, "Can you tell me?"

Reading-focused learners ask, "Is there a manual for this?"

Kinesthetic learners ask, "Can I try it myself?"

Empowering employees by understanding their strengths, triggers, and learning styles leads to better engagement and productivity.

•••

# E

# MINDSETS, PERSPECTIVES & LOYALTY

## 1. What can corporate leaders learn from marine officers?

A recent conversation with a Naval officer was really enriching, because I felt that the corporate world can pick up so many lessons from this domain. This would be useful to get the best results for individuals and organizations. Here are a few takeaways from that conversation:

1. **Sea legs:** the infrastructure inside a warship and submarines is not big enough, especially the ladders that take you from one level to another. They are steep, and early in the training, most of the officers are not able to move swiftly on the ladders. Some may feel dizzy; some may fall and some of them may not be able to climb up or down swiftly for a long time. However, as their training progresses over time, they are able to move swiftly without falling down. Their seniors would often check with them by asking, "Do you have the sea legs now?" Likewise, in the corporate world, when people are new in the organization, they may not have the necessary skills to navigate in the workplace. As leaders or managers, how do you check in with your team members?

2. **Rule of three:** While climbing the ladders inside the ship, it is a rule that three out of four limbs have to be in contact with the ladder; otherwise, one can slip or fall down. Likewise, in the corporate world, individuals must focus on having head, heart, and actions aligned to have the best results. Easier said than done, with more awareness, one can focus on getting this alignment.
3. **Teamwork:** Teamwork is extremely important when working on board ship. Helping the smooth running of a vessel and getting its work completed needs people in various roles and disciplines, including those ashore. None of the roles is big or small; for smooth sailing, everyone must believe in the power of teamwork. The most effective teamwork happens when individual team members harmonize their efforts and work toward a common goal. Effective teamwork is vital in order to reap the rewards of higher productivity, fewer internal struggles, and a more enjoyable work experience. Likewise, this applies to corporate life as far as teamwork is concerned.

**Are you practising any of these and what has been your experience?**

# 2. Using the Power Interest Grid for Managing Stakeholders

Irrespective of the industry that you work in, many of us have to work with different stakeholders to achieve collaborative outcomes. Stakeholder Management is an important discipline that successful people use to win support from others. It helps them ensure that their projects succeed where others might fail. Stakeholder Analysis is the technique used to identify the key people who have to be won over. You then use Stakeholder Planning to build the support you actively need when needed.

### Benefits of Using a Stakeholder-Based Approach

- You can use the opinions of the most powerful stakeholders to shape your projects at an early stage. Their input can also improve the quality of your project.
- Gaining support from powerful stakeholders can help you win more resources, making it more likely that your projects will be successful.
- By communicating with stakeholders early and frequently, you can ensure that they fully understand what you are doing and the benefits of your project. This means they can support you actively when necessary.

### Prioritize Your Stakeholders

Once you have the long list of people and organizations that are affected by your work, some of them may have the power to block or advance your project. Some may be interested in what you are doing, while others may not care. This is where the Power-Interest Grid helps to segment and prioritize stakeholders. Doing this helps to identify stakeholders based on their power and interest in the project.

When you plot your stakeholders on a power/interest grid, you can determine who has high or low power to affect your project, and who has high or low interest.

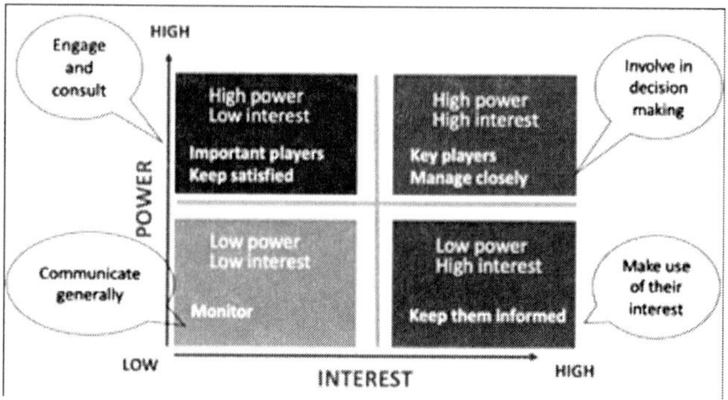


**How to Use the Power-Interest Grid**

- High Power, Low Interest – They must be kept happy, but they won't be as concerned about the details of your project.
- High Power, High Interest – These groups are influential and should be kept informed regularly.
- Low Power, High Interest – They have little say in the outcome of your project, but because they're deeply invested, you should carefully address their concerns.
- Low Power, Low Interest – This group is the most hands-off. You should monitor them without overwhelming them with too much information.

**Go ahead and use the #PowerInterestGrid to navigate your journey with different stakeholders effectively!**

## 3. Theory Y for Encouraging Employee Loyalty

'Khelo je jaan se' is a philosophy designed by an organization, which means people are expected to give their best and perform better than last year. Every year, individuals set goals for themselves and work towards achieving them.

This philosophy is based on Theory Y. Theory Y management style is based on a more optimistic view of human nature and assumes the following:

- Work is as natural as play or rest. People want to and can be self-directed and self-controlled and will try to achieve organizational goals they believe in.
- Workers can be motivated using positive incentives and will try hard to accomplish organizational goals if they believe their efforts will be recognized and rewarded.
- Under proper conditions, the average person not only accepts responsibility but seeks it out. Most workers have a relatively high degree of imagination and creativity and are willing to help solve problems.

**What do you think are the potential disadvantages of this approach?**

## 4. Understanding mindsets to help team members grow

My elder son is doing well in his academics and my younger son is average in his academics. One of the main differences I see is the approach they have towards their work. The elder one feels that his abilities, intelligence, and talents as innate traits are the key determinants of his success.

He thinks that success is a result of these inherent qualities rather than effort, and he avoids challenges that could lead to failure or reveal his perceived limitations.

On the other hand, my younger son feels that talents and abilities can be developed through dedication, hard work, and persistence. He tends to embrace challenges, persist in the face of setbacks, see effort as the path to mastery, and learn from feedback.

If, in some tests, the elder one doesn't get good scores, he gives up. On the other hand, my younger one has been working on the feedback he has received from his teacher and diligently working on it. Progress has been evident over a period of time, because he didn't give up. Two kids with different mindsets—quite a challenge for a parent!

**As a leader, what steps are you taking to understand the mindsets of your team members and help them grow?**

## 5. From Telling to Asking: The Leadership Shift That Drives Engagement

Case in point: While interacting with a customer service manager recently, I noticed that he immediately got into a telling mode and provided solutions, which I was not clearly interested in. While this 'telling' went on for some time, when he ran out of solutions, he asked me, "Do you have suggestions or thoughts for this challenge?"

Inviting thoughts and suggestions from the other stakeholder creates a space of exploration and possibilities. It also demonstrates the intention to seek opinions of others and involve them in the decision-making process. Asking the right questions is the key.

**For a leader, making the shift from a telling style to an asking style can be a big game-changer!** I have personally experienced this in my career, when I worked with a 'telling' leader versus an 'asking' leader, and the impact it had on me from an engagement perspective

**Are you aware of your style and its impact on your team members?**

•••

# SECTION 2: CASE STUDY

# A

# TEAM AND ROLE DYNAMICS

## 1. Case Study: Navigating Team

Neeraja, Social Media Manager at Waldorf Ltd, was having a tough time with her colleague, Shyam, who used to 'appear busy' all the time, but did not really contribute effectively to achieve work outcomes on time.

As a co-founder of the organization, Shyam loved to strategize and have an umbrella perspective; however, executing deliverables on time was an area where he acutely struggled. Although he was aware of his developmental areas, he would not speak up about the same with his team members, for fear of being judged. And Neeraja, too, struggled to convey her thoughts in a straightforward way, since she feared hurting the co-founder.

He struggled a lot in prioritizing work and believed that for a designer, it was difficult to deliver within fixed deadlines to create an 'excellent design'. Before joining this organization as a co-founder, Shyam was freelancing as a graphic designer. As a freelancer, he could choose his projects and negotiate timelines of deliverables. As a co-founder, he was responsible for both strategizing and execution, since it was a small team. Having a fixed mindset largely put him in a defensive mode, and it started impacting his connections and credibility with the team.

This attitude was not only hampering the work outcomes but was also creating work overload and frustration for Neeraja too. Since there was interdependence in their work, Neeraja was feeling infuriated because they both were held accountable.

**Share your approach which Neerja should take in this scenario**

____________________________________________

____________________________________________

____________________________________________

____________________________________________

____________________________________________

•••

## 2. Case Study: L & D programmes: Building a Supportive Workplace

Do you know the top L&D Programs that top Indian firms are running to upskill their employees?

**Axis Bank:** The leading private sector bank recently teamed up with Coursera to offer world-class learning programs to its employees. The course offers training in subjects such as data analytics, leadership, innovative thinking and more. These courses are being offered by some of the top universities across the globe and all Axis Bank employees are encouraged to take up the course.

**Infosys:** Infosys has power programs to upskill their employees. It was one of the first companies to offer a hike if the employees reskilled in emerging tech. Its bridge programmes skill young talents who have spent a minimum of three years in the organization to get trained in areas such as consulting, full-stack development, power programming, tech architecture and more. The aim is to provide employees with alternate career growth instead of their leaving organizations for further studies. It offers a salary rise of 80-120% to those who upskilled.

**Oracle:** The company offers a wide range of technical and professional courses in the form of online learning. They offer reimbursement for selected job-related training and education. Oracle also encourages job-related advanced degrees and continuing education while employees are employed. It works closely with Stanford Center for Professional Development (SCPD) to upskill its employees.

**TCS:** TCS runs multiple initiatives to help employees grow in their careers. Some of these programmes are Career Hub, which provides TCS employees with mentoring services. They also run Inspire, a specialized program that provides fast-track career progression to high-potential employees.

**Terence:** The company focuses strongly on enabling its employees to get a stronger foothold in analytics. With its Gateway programme, it helps employees with aptitude in analytics and provides a platform to clarify doubts, seek direction, and interact with professionals with hands-on experience in the analytics space. It also has an initiative known as 'U Learn V Pay', which encourages employees to learn from online coaching platforms, where the entire fee is reimbursed on successful completion of the course.

**Wipro**: Wipro School of Decision Sciences is aimed at data science transformation, providing tech-stack enabled programmes for employees to train on a variety of skills. In this six-month-long course, it helps employees to get equipped with skills such as data, algorithms, modelling, visualisation and more. Wipro has also announced the launch of 'WiSTA – Data Scientist' program in India, an integrated post-graduate programme in analytics. It aims at creating an industry-ready cadre of data scientists within Wipro in the information management and analytics space.

**As a leader, what steps are you taking to ramp up your team members' learning?**

________________________________________

________________________________________

________________________________________

________________________________________

________________________________________

•••

## 3. Case Study: Enhancing Team Engagement

Managing stakeholder expectations is crucial for the success of any project. It requires a strategic approach that includes identifying and analyzing stakeholders, understanding their needs and expectations, and creating a stakeholder engagement plan.

Here is an interesting real-time case between three stakeholders (A European Architect, an Indian Project Manager, and an Indian Lighting Consultant) who were working for an Indian Construction firm.

The European Architect recommended that they should experiment with global colors for the lighting (more subtle tones of color). On the other hand, the Lighting Consultant felt that they should use bold and bright colors so that the building stands out.

Now the Indian Project Manager had the tough job of bringing in alignment of thought between these two key stakeholders. He and his team created a palette of Indian colors and shared the same with the European Architect to convince him about the preference of colors in an Indian urban setting (that they needed to be a bit more vibrant, than what he had suggested) and on the other hand, the Indian lighting Consultant had to be convinced to tone down in his taste and preference of lighting colors, since he was suggesting brighter colors.

After meeting these two key stakeholders independently, the Indian Project Manager called for a combined meeting with both of them where they were ready to listen to different perspectives and what the client really wanted. The meeting concluded on a positive note where the Indian Project Manager could influence them 'think globally but to act loyally'.

Managing and influencing stakeholders can be a herculean task if one is not aware of the ways to get them aligned. You need to make them a 'hero' in their story, and along the way inspire, influence and negotiate with them to get them aligned.

**Lessons Learned**

_______________________________________________

_______________________________________________

_______________________________________________

_______________________________________________

_______________________________________________

•••

# B

# LEADERSHIP STYLES & COMPASSION

## 1. Case Study: Am I a compassionate leader?

What you give, the universe returns it to you manifold! This is the law of the universe! And if one is doing good consistently, what more can one ask for!

Here's a story of a leader, Prakash, who was a compassionate leader. He was working in the Middle East where the majority of his team members were Indians too. Since many of them were away from their motherland, they used to frequently receive parcels from home, which they wanted to collect as soon as possible. Now sometimes, the timings to collect their parcels were during office hours, and Prakash used to tell his team members that they could go, but they should be ready to work overtime, in case there was any pending work. The team members readily agreed to this arrangement, which served both purposes: completing work on time and keeping team members happy. This approach continued for many months.

After three months, the Finance Head raised a query why Prakash's team was not asking for overtime payment, even though they were working overtime.

Prakash didn't have any answer. He rushed to his team and asked them for an answer. He was stumped to listen to their response: "We are very grateful to you because you stood by us in our time of need. Now it is our time to express our gratitude." Prakash was almost teary-eyed with this gesture!

Every leader has his/her style of leading people—sometimes consciously and at times not so consciously. As a leader, what steps or actions are you taking to practice compassionate leadership?

**Share your response**

________________________________________

________________________________________

________________________________________

________________________________________

________________________________________

•••

## 2. Case Study: Creating a sense of belongingness

What are the most common practices for celebrating the birthdays of your employees?

- Personalized gifts, greeting cards, and cake.
- Talk about their achievements.
- Decorate their desk.
- Adventurous activities/team activities
- Shoutout on social media
- Gift them gift vouchers so that they can select their gift.
- Give them a health insurance policy, gym membership, or wellness kit on their birthdays.

- Professional development opportunity
- Memory lane photo collage
- Organize competitions.

Here is a story of a leader who went one step further and decided to surprise his team members by curating a special practice for their families. In this practice, a team member used to visit the family of another team member to understand their food preferences (veg/non-veg) and make a note of their favourite dishes. On the birthday of that employee, the entire family would be surprised by a meal for all from the organization. To the delight of every employee, he followed this practice for many months.

What do you think would be the impact of this on the employees and his/her family?

**Lessons Learned**

___________________________________________

___________________________________________

___________________________________________

___________________________________________

___________________________________________

•••

## 3. Case Study: Can a leader disrupt and positively influence team members who have been stuck in their roles for a long time?

Prakash, who has been recently transferred to be the Centre Director of Galaxy mall, was spending time in the initial few days to understand his team members. He realized that there were 3 team members who were stuck in Operations, Sales and Marketing roles respectively for a period of almost 7 years and were now absolutely in their comfort zone. He felt it is essential to move them out of their comfort zone to unleash their true potential. He would have to disrupt this status quo by doing role transfers. His announcement of the role transfers met with resistance for obvious reasons.

To get their buy-in Prakash decided to have one-on-ones with each of them to help them uncover their strengths and weaknesses. He also started sharing stories and best practices from his own experiences, seeking their inputs to improvise the current processes and systems. Initially, the journey started with a lot of reluctance, slowly they started doing a few things unhappily, and over a period of time they started realizing the positive impact of their small steps and actions that they took and hence started doing them with some ownership.

Prakash started acknowledging and appreciating this change in behavior publicly; hence, they felt motivated to repeat those behaviours. Steady handholding and grooming them wholeheartedly helped them realize there was no fun in sticking in the same role for many years and that it is essential to embrace change use Prakash's guidance, and unleash their potential. When this realization hit them, the mindset shift happened, and they took up complete ownership of their responsibilities which brought out great outcomes. They themselves were surprised looking back that they had been able to do this. However, they were grateful to Prakash for disrupting their status quo and help them grow in their respective careers.

## Lessons Learned

•••

C

# COMMUNICATION & ONE-ON-ONE PRACTICES

## 1. Case study: Is it necessary to have one-on-ones?

**I am coming from a start-up culture mindset, and I don't believe in having one-on-ones!** Clearly, initiating one-on-ones with his team members was a challenge for this young leader, Rohit.

Rohit came from a strong technical background and 'managing people' as a concept was totally new for him. The root of his challenge was his mindset. After an introspection exercise on 'leadership mindset', he became more aware of his feelings of being overwhelmed with managing a team and listening to their challenges, hand-holding them, etc.

I suggested to him to block time every month with one of his team members and have a one-on-one with them, rather than random one-on-ones. This would help him to prepare for the one-on-ones beforehand. However, he shared his next challenge by saying 'I need a structure for a one-on-one conversation, otherwise it just spreads over.' As his challenge was slowly unraveling itself, I asked him what could be some ways in which he could structure it. After a thoughtful pause, he suggested crafting an agenda for every one-on-one so that a structure gets created. I also suggested to him to keep the agenda slightly flexible in case new things come out of that conversation.

This was the starting point of his journey to initiate one-on-ones with his team members. With some more hand-holding and practice came more refinement and confidence, not only in the structure and frequency but also the quality of his one-on-ones.

**Lessons Learned**

________________________________________

________________________________________

________________________________________

________________________________________

________________________________________

•••

# SECTION 3: ACTIVITY

# CULTURE & ENGAGEMENT SCORECARD

Objective: Evaluate and enhance workplace culture and employee engagement strategies.

Instructions:

1. Daily Observations:

- How engaged did my team seem today? (Rate 1-10)
- Did I recognize or appreciate someone's effort?
- How did I handle conflicts or disagreements?
- Did I create a positive and inclusive environment?

2. Self-Assessment:

- At the end of the week, analyze engagement scores.
- Identify trends in team morale and engagement.

3. Reflection Questions:

- What motivates my team the most?
- What signs of disengagement did I notice?

- How can I improve communication and recognition next week?

Why This Activity?

- Enhances understanding of workplace culture.
- Helps managers proactively address disengagement.
- Encourages a more people-focused leadership approach.

•••

# PART 4
# COACHING & MENTORING

# INDEX

# SECTION 1: CHAPTERS

# A

# COACHING FOUNDATIONS & LEADERSHIP

## 1. Leader as a coach

Have you seen a leader who cares to focus on leveraging the employee's potential by putting on a 'coach's hat?

As a leader-coach, you should focus on helping individuals improve their performance by identifying and addressing interference factors, as well as developing strategies to increase potential. Here are some interesting ways:

1. **Identify Interference Factors:** A coach can help individuals identify the factors that are limiting their performance. This can be done through observation, feedback, and self-reflection. For example, a coach may notice that an athlete is consistently underperforming during competitions and may identify stress as a possible interference factor.

2. **Develop Strategies to Reduce Interference:** Once interference factors have been identified, a coach can help individuals develop strategies to reduce or eliminate them. For example, a coach may work with an athlete to develop relaxation techniques to manage stress.

3. **Increase Potential:** In addition to reducing interference, a coach can help individuals increase their potential by developing their skills and abilities. This can be done through training, feedback, and goal setting. For example, a coach may work with an athlete to develop a training plan that focuses on improving their weaker areas.

In conclusion, an individual's performance is equal to his or her potential minus interference. While interference factors can never be completely eliminated, a leader-coach can help individuals identify and reduce interference, as well as increase their potential. By working with a coaching mindset, individuals can achieve higher levels of performance and reach their full potential.

**As a leader, do you put on the 'coach's hat' to identify interruptions and help your team members utilize their full potential?**

•••

## 2. 360-Degree Feedback

To identify future leaders, among a group of high performers, I recently completed a series of coaching conversations using a 360-degree feedback report with a group of managers. Here are some experiences from the entire exercise:

1. There were a couple of managers who took full ownership of this exercise, in terms of proactively identifying their strengths and development areas and created their IDPs (individual development plans). They needed to bounce their ideas off me and validate their thoughts in terms of their growth journey.
2. Few managers were aware of their development areas; however, they seemed to be still in the 'denial' mode, unwilling to take the most discomforting steps in terms of owning it. Their 'blind spots had a surprising aspect and on the face of it, they mentioned that they would seek further feedback from different stakeholders on these areas.
3. Some managers were still in the middle range, wherein they knew their strengths and development areas; however, they didn't have insights into leveraging strengths or managing developmental areas. The conversations were more about 'what they could possibly do differently' to take their learning journey ahead.
4. An interesting case of a manager who almost evaded coming for this one-to-one debriefing conversation twice. The reasons could be many; however, the reality was that he never bothered to inform anyone as well! The highest form of non-ownership!

5. In yet another engaging conversation, a lady shared how she had grown in the ranks, right from being a steno, to managing high-value projects by interacting with stakeholders across various departments, just because she had the sincerity, focus, and determination along with the support of her seniors to grow in her career.

While different organizations invest in different ways to identify leadership potential and coach employees, how the employees are also utilizing that opportunity to leverage their potential was an interesting insight for me through this exercise! **Whether you are 'coachable' is one of the key determinants in making the coaching journey meaningful for you!**

•••

## 3. Structuring an effective reverse mentoring program

In the last few years, in many companies I have seen three generations working together — and it'll continue as youngsters join the workforce while older workers opt to extend their careers. By making reverse mentoring a part of your company culture, you can reduce generational gaps that appear now and in the future. It is important to remember the following pointers to create a structure for the reverse mentoring program:

Have clear roles and expectations. It's easy for a senior leader to change the conversation from "I'm here to learn from you" to "here's some advice."

Ensure junior employees feel safe to share. Senior leaders who act as mentees should preface the relationship by explaining that the advice is to help them gain a new perspective. You don't want junior employees to think sharing critical feedback will damage their careers.

Have mentees (leaders) follow up with their mentors about impact. It's frustrating to put effort into something and never see the results. If leaders take lessons from their sessions but don't share how it impacts company policy or strategy, it's not very encouraging to junior employees. Instead, leaders should go to their mentors and let them know how their advice spurred changes in the business.

It's also a good idea to set schedules and communication channels for mentors and mentees to meet. This way, there's consistency and convenience on both ends. For instance, participants in PwC's reverse mentoring program meet quarterly to discuss issues. Others may do monthly one-hour sessions, in person, or via webcam.

As you build a reverse mentorship program, choose mentors and mentees carefully. Consider the goals of the company then identify the knowledge gaps in leadership and which junior employees can help fill them.

To make the most of the mentorship, mentors should ask mentees questions to learn more about their gaps. Examples of reverse mentoring questions include:

- What roadblocks do you have in understanding younger customers or colleagues?
- What tools do you struggle to use for work?
- What are your key struggles with learning about Gen Z (or other topics)?
- What are some things you'd like to learn about (subject)?
- What experiences have you had with (subject) in the past?
- How are you dealing with the changes presented by (subject)?

Creating a structure, clarifying purpose, addressing challenges (biases in the workplace and conflicts between different generations) are some of the important pointers that will help you in implementing a successful 'reverse mentoring program'.

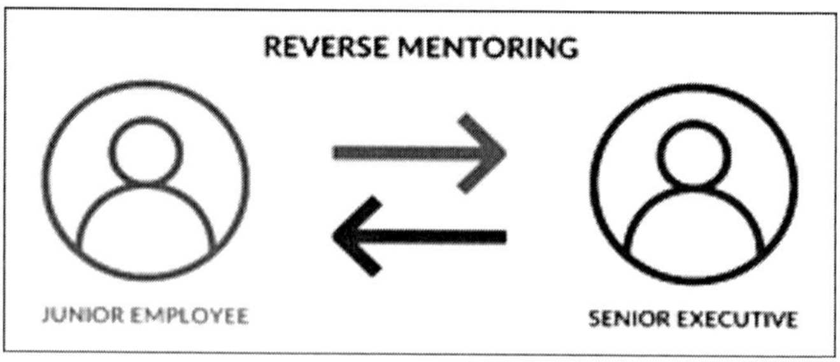


•••

## 4. Fear of failure

In a coaching conversation recently, the coach shared that one of the biggest demotivators in his career has been 'fear of failure'. He felt very emotional when his motivation report also highlighted the same. It was almost a deep realization for him that it was high time that he took some solid action on this. Our conversation eventually went on to what and how to address this.

Fear of failure (also known as "atychiphobia") is fear that stops us from doing the things that help us move forward to achieve our goals. He confessed that many times even when he is performing the simplest of tasks at work, he feels the fear of failure deeply. Because of this, he sometimes also makes mistakes!

**What causes this fear of failure?**

1. Some people develop this fear in childhood due to critical or unsupportive parents/teachers/family. Such children may constantly feel undermined or humiliated. They may carry those negative feelings into adulthood.
2. For some, it could be past failures, for example, a presentation that went badly, may make a person afraid of failing everywhere. The person may even carry that fear forever if not dealt with.
3. Perfectionists tend to have this fear. For them, it is all about doing everything perfectly. Anything less than perfection seems like a dismal and humiliating failure that cannot be tolerated. This fear of failure may stop us from trying altogether. No matter how golden the opportunity looks, the fear of failure again may take over, freezing the person in his/her tracks!

The coach had a history of critical parents, recent experience at the workplace where he had made a mistake in one of the presentations. So, a lot of inner work needed to be done here. Acknowledging, pausing, and reflecting on his early childhood experiences, along with recent experiences at the workplace, understanding the triggers and consciously working on it step by step, holding space for him to curate different responses from the autopilot ones he had - helped him become confident and courageous to easily face what triggered him.

While many of us know what motivates us, it is equally important to reflect on and understand what demotivates us. Sometimes, without realizing it, it has already become a roadblock in our journey hence seeking the help of a coach can be a game changer!

•••

# B

# SHAPING MINDSETS & UNLOCKING GROWTH

## 1. Nudging a different outlook

Are you a young professional who has recently joined an organization? Then this will be an interesting story for you.

Sanjay, who is a young executive freshly recruited from the campus, prefers to follow the instructions given by his manager and complete his tasks. His manager asks him to do basic tasks like taking printouts, typing reports, writing emails, completing excel sheets to fill in the database and so on. This went on for almost four months, and Sanjay felt bored and frustrated and said so to his boss.

**Sanjay:** "I am not enjoying what I am doing. Can you give me tasks that are more meaningful and where I can add value?" The manager looked at him with a dumbfounded expression and spoke.

**Manager:** "In fact, I am giving you tasks that are meaningful for you". When I ask you to type reports, do you try to read and make an effort to understand them and come and ask questions if you have any? Or when you complete the excel sheets, do you try to look at or analyze the data in any way which could be useful for our team or the organization?

Sanjay was stumped! The reality hit him hard; he was mindlessly doing tasks that he was assigned. Although he felt bad initially, he realized that the only way to learn would be by making the effort to understand the intent behind every task, what he could possibly learn from it and become better at it.

After three years of learning and growing in the role, Sanjay rose to replace his boss. His boss had gently nudged him about his mindset and coached him along the way for which he is totally grateful.

**Nudging**

•••

## 2. Turning weakness into a strength?

A 10-year-old boy wanted to learn Judo despite the fact that he had lost his left arm in a devastating car accident. The boy began training with an old Japanese Judo Sensei. He was doing well, so he couldn't understand why, in the first 3 months of training, the Master had taught him only a single move. The boy asked, "Sensei, shouldn't I be learning more moves?"

"This is the only move you know. But this is the only move you will ever know," the Sensei replied.

Not quite understanding, but believing in his teacher, the boy kept training.

Several months later, the Sensei took the boy to his first tournament. Surprising himself, the boy easily won his first two matches. The third match proved to be more difficult, but after some time, his opponent became impatient and charged. The boy deftly used his one move to win the match. Still amazed by his own success, the boy reached the finals.

This time, his opponent was bigger, stronger, and more experienced. The referee was concerned, and he called a time-out. He was about to stop the match when the Sensei intervened.

The Sensei insisted, "Let him continue."

Soon after the match resumed, his opponent made a critical mistake. He dropped his guard. Instantly, the boy used his move to pin him. The boy won the match and the tournament.

On the way home, the boy and Sensei reviewed every move in each and every match. Then the boy summoned the courage to ask what was really on his mind.

"Sensei, how did I win the tournament with only one move?"

"You won for two reasons," the Sensei answered.

"First, you've almost mastered one of the most difficult throws in all of Judo. And second, the only known defence for that move is for your opponent to grab your left arm."

The #master helped the boy turn his # biggest weakness into his # biggest strength.

As leaders/managers, can we identify and make a joint effort with our team members to help them turn their weaknesses into their strengths? Thoughts?

•••

## 3. Do your career aspirations determine your growth?

Career aspirations are an individual's vision or desired path one wants to pursue in one's work, which includes their long-term objectives, job preferences, and the level of success they hope to achieve.

Jacob was a graphic designer in an organization, and he had an aspiration to grow in his career: acquiring expertise, building his own startup, and having 30 branches around the world. Although he had a broad map charted out in his mind, he decided to take baby steps to achieve the milestones he had set for himself. Some of the important steps that he took are enumerated below:

**Making your boss's job easier:** In his day-to-day interactions with his boss, it was essential for him to dive deeper and understand tasks and projects for which he could offer help to make his boss's job easier. By taking this ownership, he would not only build his expertise but also gain the trust of his boss.

**Live the company's values:** One of his company's values was 'customer centricity'. When he consciously decided to live this value with internal and external stakeholders, he was building credibility and inspiring others to live this value too. Living the company's values also strengthened his sense of purpose.

**Be proactive and take initiative:** By going beyond his job description, Jacob would consciously take steps to embrace newer and different tasks that demonstrated his hunger to learn and grow. This would help him strengthen his capabilities and demonstrate ownership.

**Build relationships and talk about career aspirations:** In the journey of going beyond his job description, when Jacob focused on building connections with different stakeholders, he was focusing on building relationships, which has a huge pay-forward element. He would also get an opportunity to talk about his career aspirations and seek feedback, support, and guidance from them.

Everyone has their own unique life story, shaped by various experiences, influences, and ambitions. One fundamental aspect of this narrative is our career aspirations, which define our dreams and goals in the professional realm. These aspirations are like threads that interweave with the different chapters of our lives, guiding our choices and driving us toward self-fulfillment.

•••

# 4. Bridging the Gap: Aligning Team Aspirations with Abilities for Success

**What is aspiration?**

- A strong desire to achieve something high or great.
- An aspiration to become famous.

**What is ability?**

- The mental or physical power or skill needed to do something.
- She had the ability to explain things clearly and concisely.

As a leader, are you aware of the gap between the aspirations and abilities of your team members? Here's what you can do:

1. Conduct one-on-ones to understand their aspirations.
2. Conduct skill-gap analysis to assess your team's current skills and compare them with the skills required for their roles and goals. You can use various methods to assess your team's skills, such as self-evaluation, peer feedback, performance reviews, skill tests, or online tools.
3. Supporting them with resources, tools and training to bridge the gap between their current skills and required skills.
4. With role-transfers, job rotations, coaching, mentoring, and customized training, leaders can handhold them to bridge the gap between aspirations and abilities.

Yes, it's not an overnight change, but a persistent and patient journey for both the leader and team members. Understanding and closing the gap between aspirations and abilities will take individuals, teams, and the organization to the next level.

•••

C

# MENTORSHIP AND TRANSFORMATION STORIES

## 1. Did you know the benefits of becoming a mentor?

As it relates to business, I think of a mentor as someone who helps another person grow, develop, or progress in their career. Many people begin their careers as a mentee, seeking out others who are willing to help them. But as we get older, I believe it's important to reach out and mentor younger folks, not only to help others with their careers, but also because being a mentor can help our careers too! Here are some encouraging reasons for one to be a mentor:

- Better understand the business: "My mentee helped me see issues in the company that I didn't know existed."
- Better understand how people perceive you: "I was able to see the perception others held of me, through the eyes of my mentee."
- Create a larger network: "By helping others I've also created a network of allies I can rely upon when I need help."

- Help solve issues: "I've been able to gain a broader perspective and help my mentees see things from other perspectives. This, in turn, has helped me in resolving issues within my own department."
- Personal satisfaction: "I have been able to watch and actively help younger folks succeed in our industry – and it's such a wonderful feeling to help another person succeed!"

Mentoring another person is one of the greatest gifts you give that person. And there's almost no better feeling in the world than to help another person accomplish that person's dreams. There's an unexplained karma in the world that you get what you give, and the more people you mentor, the more the rewards come back to you, multiplied.

•••

## 2. Is there a boundary between a mentor and a mentee?

Mentoring is like teaching penguins how to fly; they have wings, but they think they are only used for walking, till we teach them how to fly with them!

While a great mentorship can result in a transformative connection between two people, it requires a delicate balance of three things:

- Commitment (meeting regularly)
- Curiosity (asking thoughtful questions)
- Vulnerability (being open and honest)

**Commitment**

The 'why' of seeking a mentor must be clearly defined. Additionally, the mentor must be willing to invest time, energy, and expertise before starting the journey. It's a two-way commitment.

**Curiosity**

Asking thoughtful questions is an art, and learning this art can help the mentor have deep conversations with the mentee and facilitate the reflective and transformative process.

**Vulnerability**

Every relationship has at least four levels of communication. These levels are separate and are usually done sequentially. The levels are:

- **Fact** – Sharing a fact such as "Today is Wednesday."
- **Opinion** – Sharing your opinion about a topic such as "Wednesday is the worst day of the week."
- **Feeling** – Sharing your feelings such as "I hate Wednesdays."

- **Transparency** – Sharing that "I have difficulty with Wednesdays because it reminds me of my father's recent death."

While it's okay to set boundaries, the real transformation happens when the conversations reach the 'Transparency' level. With work and life overlapping in so many areas, it's nearly impossible to discuss one without tapping into the other. In most mentorships, both parties are already walking a fine line between the personal and professional.

**What's your take on the relationship between mentors and mentees?**

•••

## 3. Can a 10th-fail office boy be hired as the Purchase Manager of an organization?

For the last 6 months, Raju, an office boy, was working in Perakit Enterprises. The Sales Manager, Suhas, in this organization, casually asked Raju if he was really enjoying the work he did? To which he said 'no'. He mentioned that he had the desire to become an officer one day in a reputed organization. However, when Suhas asked about his educational qualifications, Raju mentioned that he had not completed his school and had failed in the 10th grade. Suhas emphasized that completing his school and college education would be a definite step for him to become an officer in a reputed organization, and also to start learning basic computer skills. He asked Raju if he was willing to put in these efforts. And Raju replied in affirmation.

When Suhas saw the willingness in Raju, he encouraged and guided him in his studies and examinations, which enabled him to clear his 10th exam in the following year. As he sought admission to a college later, he also guided Raju to learn basic computer skills (word and excel to begin with). While continuing with his college education, Raju enthusiastically learnt computer skills, and started supporting the finance team by completing the Excel sheets. Over a period of time, he became confident in completing such tasks. After a year or so, he started observing the conversations of the Purchase Manager with different stakeholders, to learn the tricks of the trade. The Purchase Officer would also answer Raju's queries whenever he had any. After about a year and a half, this Purchase Officer had submitted his resignation. Before resigning both he and Suhas had recommended that Raju should be considered for this position. Raju was indeed ready to take up this new role, not only armed with his education, but also with great guidance, support, and coaching by Suhas and the earlier Purchase Officer.

Many a time, managers have to wear a 'coaching' hat to groom their team members, and if managers are trained on coaching skills, the results will be beneficial not only for the team member but also for the organization.

•••

# D

# REVERSE MENTORING IN ACTION

## 1. Reverse Mentoring: Bridging Generations and Fostering Mutual Growth in the Workplace

### What is Reverse Mentoring?

Reverse mentoring is a form of peer-to-peer coaching where junior employees offer mentorship to senior leaders. Jack Welch, former CEO of General Electric, first coined the term in the early 1990s after realizing the importance of the internet for businesses. A reverse mentoring program doesn't always have to be with a younger employee and an older manager. It's about the experience level of the individual in a specific skill or area.

For instance, a 45-year-old salesperson who recently made a switch to marketing can teach his or her 30-year-old manager about sales software. Or a 40-year-old Black employee might mentor a 35-year-old White manager about microaggressions in the workplace.

### Benefits of Reverse Mentoring

1. Bridge Generational Gaps

As Gen Z and Gen Alpha (the newest generation) enter the job market, ensuring a connection between the generations will be crucial to maintaining a collaborative workplace. Reverse mentoring enables companies to prioritize knowledge-sharing and keep communication and teamwork thriving in the face of social and technological differences.

2. Enable Learning (on Both Sides)

In a reverse mentoring relationship, both the mentor and mentee benefit from the experience.

**For mentees, they can learn about:**

- New technologies, such as cryptocurrency, NFTs, and social networking.
- Different cultures and demographics, particularly those they engage with in the workplace or advertise too.
- New communication styles, like adopting Slack (and even emoji and chat etiquette) vs. relying on emails or phone calls.

**For mentors, they can develop:**

- Leadership skills, which may be a boon for their career.
- Ways to identify and address generational or cultural roadblocks in the workplace.
- How to communicate with senior leaders without fear or prejudice.

Although the benefits are multifold, applying this concept in your organization can have its own challenges.

Think it through well before executing it.

## 2. Reverse Mentoring

Are you curious to know which companies in India have adopted the 'Reverse Mentoring' program?

What are the benefits they are gaining from this exercise?

**1. PepsiCo India**

PepsiCo India launched YCom — a forum of millennials elected by their own peers — as a parallel board to the executive committee. The aim was to ensure that Generation Y has a strong say in decisions that shape the company's future. Since then, YCom has been working on various areas, including reverse mentoring the executive committee on digital technologies.

Sudipto Mozumdar, Vice President of India Franchise Commercial Unit at PepsiCo, along with six other committee members, attended one such session on online productivity tools. The YCom initiative has been so successful that PepsiCo is considering replicating it in other markets, said Rajendra.

**2. GSK Consumer Healthcare India**

"We have embedded reverse mentoring in our culture, and it has a double benefit. With this, senior leaders are able to stay on the pulse of trends, while our employees feel more connected and invested because they are contributing to the improvement of their company.

**3. Vodafone India**

In its attempt to become a truly digital workplace, Vodafone India has deployed a reverse-mentoring program called Digital Ninja. As part of this, selected millennials reverse mentor the senior leadership, including the executive committee and business heads, on various digital tools.

### 4. Mindtree

At Mindtree, reverse mentoring works in a slightly different way, as part of the onboarding process for campus recruits. Rishin Chakraborthy, Program Director at Mindtree Kalinga, the IT firm's global learning Center, said that when new batches join, senior leaders, including CEO Rostow Ravanan and Chief Operating Officer Parthasarathy NS, spend time interacting with them in groups.

Over 2,400 engineering and MBA graduates have been part of this program in the last two years, and the process has cascaded throughout the organization.

### 5. Bharti Airtel

Since most of Bharti Airtel's top officials are in their 40s and 50s, the company launched a reverse mentoring program titled Rock On. All senior members were assigned a mentor, who taught them everything from how to use new gadgets to where to dine and what was trending on the internet.

Informal settings like a café or a weekend get-together at the house of the senior executive were chosen for mentoring sessions. Initial sessions served as icebreakers, where the duo discussed their likes and dislikes, favorite holiday destinations, hangouts, etc.

"I learned many new things that helped in strategizing our business. Youth use different tools to express their feelings, such as blogging or social networking sites. Earlier, the only way to gather customer feedback was to get records from our call centers. We mostly ignored blogs and social networks, from which we could have obtained endless information."

— K Srinivas, President of Bharti Airtel's Telemedia Services, quoted in The Week after being mentored by Saurab Sharma in his firm.

While the success rate of reverse mentoring is yet to be quantified, many companies in India have taken the plunge into reverse mentoring and reaped its benefits in terms of retention, diversity, and building more collaboration across generations at the workplace.

# SECTION 2:
# CASE STUDY

A

# OVERCOMING BARRIERS & SELF-LIMITING BELIEFS

## 1. Case Study: Are you aware of your self-limiting beliefs?

1. What three things do you think you could improve about yourself?

2. If you had no fears in life, what would you do differently?

Recently, my boss asked me these uncomfortable questions and although it was a difficult conversation, it helped me realize that I have been in the comfort zone for a long time and I need to become aware of some of my strongly held self-limiting beliefs and work on them. As a leader, I realized that today these beliefs are not serving me.

These beliefs have been formed over a period of time when I have heard statements from my parents and elders in the family—'tum ye mat karo' (you don't do this), or 'What if you commit any mistakes?' Since my elders didn't trust me easily, listening to these statements in my growing-up years, I grew up with the belief that I shouldn't trust others easily. Because of this belief, most of my conversations with my team members were laced with skepticism and this also kept the team members at a distance from me.

When my boss asked me the above questions, it got me thinking. During the coaching conversations, I realized that these beliefs are not helping in my personal or professional contexts, and I need to drop these beliefs. While it was not an easy journey, the self-awareness drove me to take the required actions, since I wanted different outcomes in life.

Today when I have to delegate work to my team members, I know that I have a more open mindset and am okay with allowing them to make mistakes. I need to trust them and handhold them so that they also believe in their capabilities and grow in their careers.

It is still work in progress; however, I am glad I chose to do this inner work, and it is helping me in many ways!

**Are you aware of your self-limiting beliefs?**

___

___

___

___

___

•••

## 2. Case study: Building accountability through coaching

Priya started the weekend frustrated. On Wednesday morning, she had asked Rakesh to have his team draft an executive summary about an emerging challenge for senior management. Based on feedback from her own coach, Priya was working on being clearer with her team about action items, deadlines and the reasons behind them.

With that in mind, on Wednesday, she told Rakesh that she wanted a two-page draft no later than the end of the day Friday. She and Rakesh discussed an outline for the summary, with key points to incorporate. Priya told Rakesh she planned to finalize the summary over the weekend, so her boss would have it Monday morning. Priya felt pleased by her clarity, and expected good outcomes based on the discussion.

The end of Friday came, so Priya wrote an email to Rakesh to check on the status. Rakesh acknowledged that his team had given him a draft by noon, but he had not had time to look at it before the end of the day, and he needed to log off for a family event. Rakesh attached the unreviewed draft summary to the email, "just in case you need it now."

Priya was irritated. Of course, she needed it now! She had clearly explained on Wednesday that she would be working on it over the weekend, and Rakesh's lack of focus on a mission-critical item seemed irresponsible. She opened the draft Rakesh had forwarded and became even more irritated. The document was full of technical jargon and was three pages long — a full page longer than her instructions. It was going to take hours to fix it.

Priya considered a few options:

1. Insist that Rakesh take responsibility for the project, directing him to review the draft and send her his final version by noon Saturday. While this would contradict Priya's commitment to work-life balance, Rakesh needed the pain of the negative consequence, so he would not make the same mistake again.
2. Write to senior leadership, communicating a delay in the executive summary, so Priya would not have to spend her own time on the project over the weekend, and so Rakesh could "right the ship" upon returning to work on Monday.
3. Finalize the executive summary over the weekend, as promised to senior leadership. Share the revision with Rakesh and set up a coaching/feedback session on Monday to discuss the problems and what should be done differently next time – both regarding the timeline and the document itself.

Pause and think about how you would address this if you were Priya. Would you have pursued one of these options? What other options do you see? What would you have done?

**Share your response**

________________________________________

________________________________________

________________________________________

________________________________________

________________________________________

•••

# B

# COACHING DYNAMICS & SHIFTS

## 1. Case Study: The Bridge between Coach and Coachee

Often when the coachee says "I don't know" they really do know—they're just unwilling to acknowledge or face the answer. If it was easy to say aloud, they would have done so. There can be many reasons for the "I don't know", but if we trust our instincts and explore gently—we may just be rewarded with an Aha moment!

There are any number of reasons for that "I don't know"—but most of them are probably a fear of the consequences of stating that answer aloud. Maybe it means they will need to acknowledge some change is needed in their lives (they might have to quit their job) or maybe they don't trust us enough yet and are afraid of what we will think. It could be that they're afraid of what their inner critic will say to their answer (don't be such a baby!). Or maybe it's something else.

Yet when we face that thought, that feeling, and say, "I know I need to quit my job but I'm afraid" or "I feel like such a child, but I don't want to apologize" or "I'm such a coward.

I'm terrified that they won't understand and will laugh at me/ it will damage our friendship." Now we have the Truth—and something real to work with.

From here, we can look at the feelings, explore the judgments, prepare backup plans, discover new options, and MOST importantly, honor the whole person. By this, I mean honoring the parts of our clients that feel afraid, embarrassed, ashamed, or resentful—all those feelings we "shouldn't" really feel but still do.

And it's a great time to remind our clients: "Just because you FEEL or THINK it doesn't make it true."

So, here are 15 ways to respond and turn that "I don't know" into an Aha moment!

"This is a good place to start. Let's relax for a moment into this 'don't know' place."

1. Simply use silence. Don't respond at all and wait calmly for their answer.
2. "Remember that just because you answer doesn't mean you need to do anything about it."
3. You may want to use a softener before this question: "What are you pretending not to know?"
4. "I feel that too sometimes. Take a moment and let me know when you've thought of something""
5. "What if you secretly knew the answer?"
6. "So, what's underneath the 'I don't know?' What are you avoiding?"
7. "What is it like for you to not know?"
8. "How do you feel right now as you think about answering this question?"

9. "Hmm. Take a deep breath and just allow yourself to feel into the question for a second."
10. Use with caution and excellent rapport: "If I were to snap my fingers and you knew…" (snap fingers)
11. "So, if (what they don't know about) had a colour/smell/taste/sound, what would it be?"
12. "OK, so what if you were to give me an approximate answer or a range?"
13. "Hmm. Let's try something here. Take a deep breath and let your unconscious mind create the answer as a picture instead of trying to make it happen."
14. Ask them for their helicopter perspective. "Imagine you're in a helicopter flying over the map of your life. What do you notice about your life from way up there? Looking down with this new perspective, how would you answer the question now?"

So, don't feel caught out by "I do not know" ever again. Have patience. Use one of these responses to inspire and you never know, it may even be **YOU** who has the aha moment!

**Lessons Learned**

________________________________________

________________________________________

________________________________________

________________________________________

________________________________________

•••

## 2. Case Study: Shifting from Start-Up Mentality to First-Generation Entrepreneur – A Leadership Journey

In a coaching conversation with an entrepreneur recently, he shared his challenge of shifting from a start-up mentality to become a first-generation entrepreneur. When I asked him to reflect on his belief systems, he realized that these beliefs were set because of his father, whom he saw as someone who was ready to take risks in business but would not let go of his power. At times he would be micromanaging too. As he was growing up, he felt that this was the best way of managing people and getting things done. Unfortunately, it was not working for him in the current work context.

The second challenge was that he was unable to delegate effectively. While scaling up was one of the steps he was planning in the near future, to become a first-generation entrepreneur, he knew that he had to work on his delegation skills. I nudged him to reflect on whether the current set of people were the right people on the bus. Would revisiting the hiring process help him to delegate better? Likewise, asking him to reflect on the way he was delegating work currently was also an eye-opener for him. (by looking at the skill and willingness of each employee and then delegating and handholding them differently).

This inside-out approach helped this entrepreneur to look at the challenge holistically. After almost six months, he could consciously choose a different belief system wherein it was okay to share power with his people. He also reflected on his hiring process and focused on using the skill-will matrix while delegating work to his team members. Over a period of time, the team also started to grow because of a different approach used by the leader.

His journey can be summarized in the following way:

- awareness of the pushes and pulls of the change journey
- a deliberate action orientation
- aspiration to grow as an individual and as a leader
- and finally, an acceptance of the outcomes

**Lessons Learned**

________________________________________

________________________________________

________________________________________

________________________________________

________________________________________

•••

# SECTION 3: ACTIVITY

# COACHING AND MENTORING

Objective: Build coaching and mentoring skills through daily learning moments.

Instructions:

1. Identify Coaching Opportunities Daily:
    - Did I give constructive feedback today?
    - Did I help someone grow professionally?
    - Did I ask questions to encourage critical thinking?

2. Self-Assessment:
- At the end of the week, analyze coaching effectiveness.

3. Reflection Questions:
- Did I empower others to solve problems?
- How can I improve my mentoring skills?
- What impact did my coaching have on others?

Why This Activity?

- Strengthens mentorship skills.
- Encourages leaders to develop talent.
- Fosters a growth mindset.

# EPILOGUE

As you turn the final page, I hope you remember this: leadership is not a finished sculpture. It is a living, breathing craft. Some days you will shape it with clarity; other days, it will reshape you.

There will be moments when you lead boldly, and moments when you retreat, reflect, and begin again. But each of those moments is part of the larger story you are writing as a leader.

Your leadership muscle will grow in unexpected places—during a difficult conversation, a surprising success, a quiet apology, a courageous "no," or a compassionate pause.

Keep practicing.

Keep stretching.

Keep becoming.

The leader you are becoming is already on his or her way.

# MEETA KANHERE

Driven by an enduring fascination with human behaviour, she has spent over two decades exploring what truly moves people—what inspires them, what blocks them, and what unlocks their highest potential. Her journey across consulting firms and academic institutions has given her a rare vantage point into the minds of leaders and the mechanics of organizations.

A sportsperson for life, she lives by a simple philosophy: when you fall, rise, refocus, and play the next point. This spirit defines her approach to leadership development—resilient, future-facing, and anchored in possibility.

As the founder of Meraki Leadership Solutions, she coaches CEOs, founders, and emerging leaders to help them see themselves clearly, lead intentionally, and grow with purpose. Guided by emotional intelligence, deep listening, and unwavering presence, she creates spaces where insight becomes action and action becomes transformation.

When she steps away from the coaching room, she finds grounding in nature, the energy of a tennis court, and the quiet joy of time with family.

CONNECT WITH
ME ON LINKEDIN

9 789360 706838

Printed at Repro India Ltd.